REEL GAGS

REEL GAGS

JOKES,
SIGHT GAGS,
AND DIRECTORS' TRICKS
FROM YOUR FAVORITE FILMS

Bill Givens

BOOKS

RENAISSANCE BOOKS
Los Angeles

Copyright © 1998 by Bill Givens

All rights reserved. Reproduction without permission in writing from the publisher is prohibited, except for brief passages in connection with a review. For permission, write: Renaissance Books, 5858 Wilshire Boulevard, Suite 200, Los Angeles, California 90036.

Library of Congress Cataloging-in-Publication Data

Givens, Bill.
    Reel gags : jokes, sight gags, and director's tricks from your
favorite films / Bill Givens.
        p. cm.
    Includes bibliographical references and index.
    ISBN 1-58063-042-1 (trade paper : alk. paper)
    1. Motion pictures—Humor.   I. Title.
PN1994.9.G5887 1998
791.43'02'07—dc21   98-36564
                                                                    CIP

10 9 8 7 6 5 4 3 2
Design by Tanya Maiboroda

Distributed by St. Martin's Press
Manufactured in the United States of America
First Edition

CONTENTS

ACKNOWLEDGMENTS

*T*his book would not have been possible without the assistance and encouragement of my editor, the very thorough Jim Parish, all of the good folks at Renaissance Books, and my agent, Nancy Yost. I'm also grateful for the contributions of several friends, many of whom offered material in casual conversation even though, given the sorry state of my short-term memory, I didn't write them down for a proper acknowledgment. You know who you are, and I hope you know how much I appreciate you. I'm especially grateful to the thousands of readers of my *Film Flubs* books who have written to me over the years to share not only their favorite movie goofs, but also inside jokes and other fascinating behind-the-scenes information. Hopefully I'll be able to answer your letters before the end of the millenium (if not this one, then the next). A special thanks to Rosebud Givens Davis (she's my mother and no, she wasn't named for that sled); Bob and Janie Givens Miller; Reed Givens; Gloria Fisher; Rob, Jon, and MaryRea; Rosalind George; the Saturday Night Movie Club (Craig Phillips, Don Basse, Bill Wood, David Littler, Peter Ciarcia, Casey Criste, and John "J. P." Peterson); the Gottfrieds: Howard, Mary Lynn, Norah, and Elizabeth; Heiner Mohnen; Bill Warren; Leonard Maltin; Frank Cooper; the hundreds of radio talk show hosts who have made my books a continuing topic on their shows as well as the guests who call in to talk about movies, especially Dara Wells of WABC Radio, New York; and the many TV shows and their producers, especially Josh Mankiewicz and Leslie Bergman of *Dateline NBC*, for their continuing interest in my work.

IN ON THE JOKE

Every profession has its private inside jokes. Military jokers have sent recruits on missions to "find the key to the flagpole." Apprentice theatrical stagehands were once asked to "wash the gels" (the tinted gelatin formerly used to color stage lights) only to find they dissolved in water. Believe it or not, there's even inside humor at the Internal Revenue Service. Why else is the form that you fill out to protest unjust rulings named Form 911? An IRS spokesperson told newsman Bob McCormick of radio station KNX, Los Angeles, that it was a definite inside joke.

The stately Washington National Cathedral houses an inside joke. Traditionally, gargoyles are frightening figures. Perhaps that's why the Cathedral's stonemasons acknowledged that, hidden way up where you can't see it from the ground, one of the gargoyles has the face of

Darth Vader from the *Star Wars* film saga. It's a national tribute to the ecumenicity of the inside joke.

I once sent a gullible young intern on an urgent mission to an ad agency to pick up a quart of Midnight Oil. The weird thing is that I forgot to warn the agency he was on his way, and they stopped everything to look for it.

Moviemakers have found all sorts of ways to slip little jokes, trademarks, sight gags, and cameo performances into their films. It's a phenomenon you'll find just about anywhere movies are made; we've included not only American films, but jokes from British, continental European, and even Norwegian cinema in this collection.

While most inside jokes remain just that (i.e., amusements for those who are part of a particular milieu), filmdom's inside jokes are, for the most part, right out in front on the screen and waiting for discovery by a sharp-eyed, knowledgeable film fan.

By and large, these film gags are subtle and aren't intended to create an audience guffaw. Rather, they're smiles, gentle amusements, subtle giggles for friends, fans, and family of someone associated with the film. They can range from director Alfred Hitchcock's trademark appearances in his own films—a virtual wink at the audience—to obscure references, homages to filmmakers' mentors, cameos by children and other family members, self-homages to one's previous work, and digs at other directors and actors.

HOLLYWOOD TRICKSTER
*Director Robert
Zemeckis peppered
his* Back to the
Future *films with
inside jokes. (The
Blackburn Archive)*

The fun thing about catching inside jokes on the screen is they take your enjoyment (or your disdain) for the film to a deeper level. Beyond the story that's on the surface you've found something else to laugh at, to be amazed by, or at worst, something that gives you bragging rights when you talk about the film or its director and actors to your friends. You're one-up on them, just as the filmmakers thought they were a jump ahead of you when they slipped their little "gotcha" into the movie. They're a sprinkle of spice that flavors your viewing experience.

Some jokes are "so inside" they're hardly worth noting by anyone other than the person to whom they're

14

SURROUNDED BY JOKES *Doc and Marty, played by Christopher Lloyd and Michael J. Fox, are surrounded by inside jokes in all of the* Back to the Future *movies. (The Blackburn Archive)*

directed. Others are obvious, ready for just about anyone to spot; some are bitter. Witness Alfred Hitchcock's casting of Raymond Burr as Lars Thorwald in *Rear Window* (1954) because he could easily be made up to look like producer David O. Selznick, who Hitchcock felt had interfered too much in his previous films.

Others are nothing more than fun on film. While of no significance to the story of *Back to the Future* (1985), Marty McFly (Michael J. Fox) agrees to meet Dr. Brown (Christopher Lloyd) for their time travel experiment at "Twin Pines Mall." Lloyd says that farmer Peabody once owned all the land and grew pines there. When Fox goes back in time, he runs over and knocks down a pine tree on the Peabody's property. When the film ends and he returns to the mall, it's now called "Lone Pine Mall." Some gags become trademarks. Certain directors have "lucky actors" they use in most, if not all, of their films. Watch a Garry Marshall film, such as *Dear God* (1996), *Exit to Eden* (1994), *Frankie and Johnny* (1991), *Pretty Woman* (1990), *Beaches* (1988), *Overboard* (1987), *Nothing in Common* (1986), *The Flamingo Kid* (1984), or *Young Doctors in Love* (1982), and you'll see Hector Elizondo. Casting Elizondo is Marshall's way of giving his film a good luck talisman. Among the films in which the Coen Brothers (Joel and Ethan) cast their lucky actor, John Turturro, are *The Big Lebowski* (1998), *Barton Fink* (1991), and *Miller's Crossing* (1990). Turturro seems to be the charm for Spike Lee, too. He's in Lee's *Girl 6* (1996), *Clockers* (1995), *Jungle Fever* (1991), *Mo' Better Blues* (1990), and *Do the Right Thing* (1989).

John Landis has several trademarks, the most notable of which is the phrase "See you next Wednesday" which appears somewhere in most of his feature films, either as graffiti, or written on a theatre marquee, or printed on a film poster.

Horror film director Sam Raimi uses references to The Three Stooges in many of his films. Frank Capra used a bird, "Jimmy the Raven," as a talisman. Renny Harlan, who directed *Cutthroat Island* (1995), *Cliffhanger* (1993), and *Die Hard 2: Die Harder* (1990), spices his movies with references to his native Finland. Director Stanley Kubrick uses the number 114 as a cinematic trademark, popping it into unlikely places in his land-mark films.

In most cases, it's just the director, actor, or even the set designer having fun. Only in rare instances are these jokes mean-spirited. You'll find one of the meanest in *Wired* (1989), about the tragic life and death of comedian John Belushi. The sound of a helicopter can be heard when the actor playing John Landis is seen on the set of *The Blues Brothers* (1980). It's a cruel reference to the helicopter accident on the set of *Twilight Zone: The Movie* (1983).

16

ALL I WANT TO DO IS...ACT

A favorite Hollywood joke involves an interview with the late Mother Teresa. "You've done so many wonderful things," the reporter says. "If you had it to do all over again, would you follow the same path?" The holy woman looks at him and says with a beatific smile, "Actually, I always wanted to direct."

Transpose the scenario to a great director, and the answer might be, "Actually, I always wanted to act."

Of course, the king of cameos was Alfred Hitchcock (see "Where's Alfred," page 83). But modern-day filmmakers like Martin Scorsese, Steven Spielberg, and many others use their power as a film's field general to work themselves into their own films.

Sometimes, it's but an ephemeral image, as in *The Lost World: Jurassic Park* (1997), where you see the reflection of Steven Spielberg in the television set broadcasting the Cable News Network (CNN) story about the return of the dinosaurs. In the scene he's sitting on the couch eating popcorn beside the film's star, Jeff Goldblum.

You can also see Spielberg in *Indiana Jones and the Temple of Doom* (1984) as a tourist in the background during the opening scene at the airport. In *Jaws* (1975), Spielberg's is the voice you hear on Quint's (Robert Shaw) marine radio when Mrs. Brody (Lorraine Gary) tries to contact her husband on the *Orca*.

Spielberg also had a hand in the action of *Poltergeist* (1982). Tobe Hooper directed, but Spielberg was co-writer and co-producer. When the flesh is pulled from the investigator's face seen in the mirror, the hands doing the dirty deed are Spielberg's.

Similarly, in *The Third Man* (1949) the hand you think belongs to Orson Welles—playing Harry Lime—as he reaches up through a sewer grate, is really that of director Carol Reed. Welles was busy elsewhere the day the scene was shot, and so you use whatever is on hand...(so shoot me already!).

The Crown Prince of Cameos

When it comes to cameo appearances in their own films, after Alfred Hitchcock the probable successor in the genre is Martin Scorsese. Even though he's an accomplished actor in his own right, he can't resist popping into the movies he directs. A partial Scorsese "cameography" includes such appearances as:

THE GOOD SON
Director Martin Scorsese trademarks his work by casting his mother and father in many of his hit movies. (The Blackburn Archive)

19

Boxcar Bertha (1972): customer at the brothel

Mean Streets (1973): the man who shoots Johnny Boy (Robert DeNiro)

Taxi Driver (1976): the irate husband in Travis Bickle's (Robert DeNiro) cab

Raging Bull (1980): Barbizon Theatre stagehand who asks Jake LaMotta (Robert DeNiro) to go backstage

The King of Comedy (1983): TV director

After Hours (1985): operating the searchlight at Club Berlin

New York Stories (1989): man having picture taken with Lionel Dobie

The Age of Innocence (1993): photographer taking May's wedding picture

All the News That Fits the Plot

Conspiracy-meister Oliver Stone is a director for whom plot has more than one meaning, given that his recurring theme is a search for conspiracies. Look for him as a TV reporter in *Born on the Fourth of July* (1989). Appropriately, he's future rock legend Jim Morrison's film teacher in *The Doors* (1991). In *Platoon* (1986) Stone is the officer in the bunker which is destroyed by a suicide runner. In *Wall Street* (1987) you can see him on the phone during the deal-making montage.

20

The Director As Monster

Director Ivan Reitman got into the action of *Ghostbusters* (1984). His is the voice of Dana/Zuul, one of the creature transformations in the hit film.

The Director As Minister

The producer/director trio who made *Airplane* (1980) also appear in the movie. Jim Abrahams is the religious zealot at the beginning of the film, while the Zucker Brothers, David and Jerry, are air traffic controllers.

Applauding Her Own Work

Ida Lupino made a successful transition from her career as an actor to becoming one of the first women to direct films. However, when she directed the tennis-themed *Hard, Fast and Beautiful* (1951) she couldn't resist getting back in front of the camera, and made a cameo appearance, wearing sunglasses and applauding in a crowd scene about a half-hour into the film.

A Serious Commitment to Self-Promotion

Alan Parker is all over *The Commitments* (1991), about a struggling band of the same name. Not only does the director appear in the recording studio near the end of the film, but one of the audition songs is from Parker's *Fame* (1980), and a character on a bus is asked if he brought a copy of Parker's *Mississippi Burning* (1988). A cardboard cutout of Parker can be seen in the background of a scene when The Commitments are in a video store. And, wouldn't you know it, all the cassettes on the shelves are Parker films.

Fraught with Meaning

Alan Parker is back in the action in his *Evita* (1996). Given that it took many years, many scripts, and many directors to get what Leonard Maltin, one of America's leading authorities on film and author of his own *Movie and Video Guide*, now in its nineteenth update edition, calls "the world's largest music video" on screen, is there any portent to Parker's role as a frustrated film director?

They Go Bump in the Night

Terry Gilliam, who directed *Brazil* (1985), shows up in his provocative movie as the man who bumps into the main character, Sam (Jonathan Price), in the Shangri-La Tower.

Hitting It on the Nose

Roman Polanski, no stranger to trouble, is the hood who cuts Jack Nicholson's nose in his *Chinatown* (1974). It's questionable if it was for verisimilitude or vengeance,

A LITTLE TOO MUCH REALISM *In* Chinatown *(1974), not only did Roman Polanski appear in the film that he directed, but in this scene he actually cut Jack Nicholson's nose. (Photofest)*

but he actually cut Nicholson's nose in the shot. Polanski should be happy there wasn't a golf club nearby.

Was it Lynch...or Smithee?

David Lynch shows up as a radio operator in the mining ship that is rescued from a sandworm in *Dune* (1984). If you saw the television version, lengthened with unused footage from the theatrical cut, it was directed not by Lynch but by the ubiquitous Alan Smithee. If you're not familiar with Smithee's execrable work, check out his filmography on page 156.

The Director Delivers

If a film is a director's baby, David Cronenberg more than delivers. Not only did he give birth to *The Fly* (1986), he also appears as the obstetrician who delivers the maggot baby.

23

A Kiss on the Bum

Peter Jackson takes on a part in *Heavenly Creatures* (1994) that reinforces so many actors' opinion of their directors. He's the bum kissed by Juliet (Kate Winslet) outside the theatre. In *The Frighteners* (1996), he's back as the pierced and bearded man whom Frank (Michael J. Fox) bumps into before the ghost of Ray (Peter Dobson) knocks him down.

A Double Debut

John Singleton's directorial debut was *Boyz N the Hood* (1991). It also marks his debut as a Hollywood hyphenate, writer-director-actor, when he is discovered in his production playing a mailman.

Marching to His Own Beat

Garry Marshall directed the light comedy *Overboard* (1987). Look for him in a cameo role as a drummer.

Director to the Second Power

The director directs both within and without *Apocalypse Now* (1979). Francis Ford Coppola not only created the war opus, but within it he has a cameo role as a director filming a war documentary.

24

Siegel's Bluff

Director Don Siegel made cameo appearances in several of his films. You can spy him beside a hotel pool in *Edge of Eternity* (1959). He runs down a street in *Dirty Harry* (1972), and is a diner cook in *The Killers* (1964). Look for him as a man in an elevator in *Coogan's Bluff* (1968), the film which spawned the *McCloud* TV series (1970–77). He plays table tennis in *Charley Varrick* (1973). In a tribute appearance, he is a taxi driver in Phillip Kaufman's 1978 remake of *Invasion of the Body Snatchers*. Siegel directed the original sci-fi classic in 1956.

The Meter Is Running

Sam Peckinpah, a towering legend among film direc-tors—especially of the "shoot 'em up" genre—pops up in

Don Siegel's *Invasion of the Body Snatchers* (1956) as a meter reader.

Making His Own Deals

Sydney Pollack, no slouch as an actor but better known as a director, takes on the role of Michael/Dorothy's (Dustin Hoffman) harried agent in his *Tootsie* (1982).

Try...and Try...and Try Again

Legendary director John Huston is the tourist from whom Fred C. Dobbs (Humphrey Bogart) begs money three times in *The Treasure of the Sierra Madre* (1948). This masterpiece filled the family mantle with Oscars. John won for Best Director and Best Screenplay, and his father, the equally legendary actor Walter Huston, won the Oscar for Best Supporting Actor in the western.

25

Taking a Stand

Mike Figgis shows up as a mobster in his *Leaving Las Vegas* (1995); in his *One Night Stand* (1997) he's a hotel clerk.

The Cross-Dressing Director

Ed Wood, who liked to direct wearing a woman's angora sweater, had nothing on Paul Mazursky. Look for Mazursky in full drag in his *Moon over Parador* (1988). You can also see Mazursky on TV promoting a book in *Scenes from a Mall* (1991), placing an order in a restaurant in *An Unmarried Woman* (1978), and as the first guest greeted by the architect in *Tempest* (1982).

The Fall Guy

Mel Smith saved a choice role for himself in *The Tall Guy* (1989). He's the backstage drunk who offers congratulations, and then collapses.

Piloting the Picture

If a director is the picture's pilot in command, George Roy Hill took the role seriously in *The World According to Garp* (1982). Fortunately, the movie's fate was better than his is in the film. He's the pilot who crashes into Garp's house.

Piloting It into History

26

Not only did Merian Cooper co-direct the 1933 version of *King Kong* into film history, he also showed up in the ape epic as the flight commander. Ernest Schoedsack helped co-pilot both the plane and the film. He was co-director of the film and appears in the film as the flight observer.

The Director's Trick

If a director's job is to teach the cast and crew what he wants from the film, perhaps there's meaning in Charles Martin Smith's cameo in his *Trick or Treat* (1986). He slips into the shock thriller as a high school teacher.

The Director As Therapist

Filmmaker Barry Levinson has a role that's a bit more than a cameo in his *Rain Man* (1988). He has a small but

THERAPY FROM THE DIRECTOR *That's director Barry Levinson examining Dustin Hoffman's sanity in his* Rain Man *(1988). (Photofest)*

substantial part as the psychiatrist who examines Dustin Hoffman. Levinson also shows up in Robert Redford's *Quiz Show* (1994) with a dead-on performance as TV morning personality Dave Garroway. Director Martin Scorsese is also part of the *dramatis personae*, as the sponsor of the quiz show. Look closely at one of *Quiz Show*'s classroom scenes at Columbia University and you'll see an unbilled Ethan Hawke as one of the students.

Portrait of a Therapist

John Waters is the psychiatrist in his *Hairspray* (1988). In *Serial Mom* (1994) he shows up in a portrait that is carried past the camera in the school's "Bring and Buy" scene.

Tour Guide

Ken Russell appears on a tour boat at the end of his *Gothic* (1986).

They Never Stop Selling

Lawrence Kasdan works himself into a very telling role in his *Grand Canyon* (1991). He tries to interest Davis (Steve Martin) in a film project.

The Fifth Beatle

Director Richard Lester can be seen at the back of the stage when the Beatles sing "Tell Me Why" in *A Hard Day's Night* (1964).

28

Now We Know Who He Is

Even the distinguished director David Lean couldn't resist a cameo appearance. In his epic *Lawrence of Arabia* (1962) he's the man who calls to Lawrence across the Suez Canal asking, "Who are you? Who are you?"

The Director As Salesman

Frank Oz is the salesman who tries to induce Seymour (Rick Moranis) to sign a contract during the song, "The Meek Shall Inherit" in his *Little Shop of Horrors* (1986).

Piloting the Project

Rob Reiner goes to new directorial heights in his *Misery* (1990). He's the helicopter pilot.

Her Brilliant Career

Gillian Armstrong not only directed *My Brilliant Career* (1979), she shows up in a nightclub scene as a backup singer.

His Not-So Brilliant Career

Ron Howard is an annoying saxophone player in his *Night Shift* (1982).

On His Way to New Heights

John Schlesinger, who helmed the thriller *Pacific Heights* (1990) can be seen in a hotel elevator.

He Knows How to Work a Camera

Jerry Paris, director of *Never a Dull Moment* (1968) shows up in the mob comedy as a police photographer.

Are You Being Served?

John Badham is a room service waiter in his *Point of No Return* (1993).

A Repulsive Talent

Roman Polanski shows his talent for creating unusual rhythms when he plays the musical spoons in his first English-language film, *Repulsion* (1965).

Now You See Him...Now You Don't

Wes Craven pops up in *Scream* (1996) as a school janitor, hyping his previous screen work with a Freddy

Krueger sweater. In *Scream II* (1997) he has a cameo as an emergency-room doctor, but his scene ended up on the cutting room floor. Now that's some director who'd cut himself out of his own film!

FRIENDS AND RELATIONS

*D*irector Joe Dante peppered *The Howling* (1981) with film buff in-jokes, the most notable of which was that he named most of the characters for directors who helmed werewolf movies. But in-the-know audiences howled when they saw a man fishing for change in a pay-phone change return slot. Making a cameo was Dante's friend, Roger Corman, the producer who is so tight-fisted he often uses the same set for several movies.

Furthering Corman's cheapskate reputation is his walk-on in Ron Howard's *Apollo 13* (1995). This time he's complaining about the high cost of the space program.

Moments like these are an example of the ultimate inside joke: putting a friend, family member, someone closely connected to the movie, or even the person whose story is told into a shot in a manner that will entertain only the *cognoscenti*. In most cases, these appearances neither contribute to, nor take away from, the story. They're merely examples of a director, actor, or producer having a bit of fun not only with his friends and relatives, but also with audience members who are sharp enough to catch the joke.

The Cartoon Maven

In *Gremlins* (1984) a man looks at Billy's (Zach Galligan) cartoon in a bar as a Warner Bros. cartoon plays in the background. The man should know his cartoons; it's Chuck Jones, the legendary animator at Warner Bros.

As If They Needed the Work

Singer Huey Lewis turns up in director Robert Zemeckis' *Back to the Future* (1985) as a high school teacher, his appearance setting up his song, "The Power of Love." Steven Spielberg drives the pickup truck that takes Marty (Michael J. Fox) back to school in the time-travel fantasy. In *Back to the Future III* (1990) famed cinematographer Dean Cundy, director of photography on the film, takes Marty and Doc's (Christopher Lloyd) picture in the sequence set in 1885.

Son of As If They Needed the Work

Screenwriter Melissa Mathison wrote a bit part for her husband in *E.T.: The Extra-Terrestrial* (1982). Most of his scenes were cut, but he does get to play the biology teacher. You can see him with his back to the audience when he explains to the class that, "the frogs won't feel a thing." Mathison's husband is superstar Harrison Ford.

Captain Trip, Grateful to Be in the Movie

Look at the crowd scene in India in *Close Encounters of the Third Kind* (1977) and you'll see The Grateful Dead's Jerry Garcia.

Mickey in the Mosh Pit

During the PowerLine band's concert in *A Goofy Movie* (1995), you can spot Mickey Mouse in the lower-left portion of the screen immediately after the stage manager is thrown into the mega-sized DiamondVision™ screen.

33

The Road to the Circus

Bob Hope, Bing Crosby, and Dorothy Lamour made a series of "Road" movies together, so when Lamour costars in Cecil B. DeMille's *The Greatest Show on Earth* (1952), the camera pans the crowd in the circus bleachers to reveal Hope and Crosby enjoying the show.

In Time of Trial

Opera singer Eileen Farrell dubbed the voice for Eleanor Parker, who played opera diva Marjorie Lawrence, in *Interrupted Melody* (1955). Director Curtis Berhardt had a bit of fun with the casting in a later scene where Lawrence hits a high note that another singer cannot. The singer who can't hit the right note is Eileen Farrell. Thus, Farrell provides the voice for the singer who can, and is the singer who can't.

A Casting Conspiracy?

Oliver Stone's *JFK* (1991) is an account of District Attorney Jim Garrison's search for the conspirators in the Kennedy assassination. Kevin Costner plays Garrison, but the real thing can be seen in the Warren Commission scenes: Jim Garrison is Supreme Court Chief Justice Earl Warren.

Now You Know What He Looks Like

Bernard Hermann composed the music for many of Alfred Hitchcock's memorable thrillers, among them the 1956 remake of his 1934 *The Man Who Knew Too Much*. He makes a cameo at the climax, conducting the orchestra in the Royal Albert Hall. And here's a surprise: this assassination intrigue movie featured Doris Day singing *Que Sera, Sera*, which became the winner of the 1956 Oscar for Best Song.

34

I Just Met a Girl Named Maria...

The Sound of Music (1965) is the story of the singing von Trapp family and their escape from Nazi Germany. When Maria (Julie Andrews) walks through an archway singing "I Have Confidence," the real Baroness Maria von Trapp is among the women in the background.

The Punk Producer

In *Star Trek IV: The Voyage Home* (1986) associate producer Kirk Thatcher is the punk on the bus, and the song that's playing on his stereo is one he composed.

EVERYBODY GETS IN THE ACT *The laughing guy in* Torch Song Trilogy *(1988) is the author of this book. (Video screen photo, collection of the author)*

35

Torch Song Duo

Our good friend Howard Gottfried, who produced *Torch Song Trilogy* (1988) as well as such notable films as *The Hospital* (1971), *Network* (1976), and *Altered States* (1980), is the distinguished gray-haired gentleman enjoying himself at the bar in *Trilogy*. In the same film, you'll see a laughing guy with glasses in a couple of cuts during the opening credits. Look closely, it's your humble servant, the author of this book.

Pilot of the Project

When Indiana Jones is ready to escape in *Raiders of the Lost Ark* (1981), the pilot of the Flying Wing is the film's producer, Frank Marshall.

THE PRODUCER HAS WINGS *The pilot of the flying wing in* Raiders of the Lost Ark *(1981) is Frank Marshall, who produced the film. (Video screen photo, collection of the author)*

36

Precursors of Fame

Victor Fleming had some prescient casting in *Gone with the Wind* (1939). Eddie Anderson, Aunt Pittypat's (Laura Hope Crews) coachman, became Jack Benny's general factotum "Rochester." George Reeves, playing Stuart Tarleton, went on to fame as TV's Superman. Finally, the horse that Thomas Mitchell rides became even more famous as the Lone Ranger's movie horse Silver. Hi Ho!

Political Casting

Famed Marxist Leon Trotsky dabbled in the early days of American film. He was an extra in *My Official Wife* (1914). Another official wife, Patricia Ryan, later to become Pat Nixon, had a part as a ballroom dancer in *Becky Sharpe* (1935).

The Family That Acts Together...

Directors love to set up a bit of onscreen immortality for members of their families. Spike Lee made jobs for his family in *Mo' Better Blues'* (1990). In the wedding scene, it's his real-life sister Joie being given away by their joint real-life father Bill Lee (who also scored the film).

Ron Howard's mom plays Jim Lovell's (Tom Hanks) wheelchair-bound mother in *Apollo 13* (1995). Howard also created work for several other members of his family. Brother Clint is one of the Houston Mission Control specialists, and father Rance Howard plays a priest. The director even worked one of the real astronauts into his space thriller: Jim Lovell is an officer on an aircraft carrier in the final sequence, and Lovell's wife Marilyn is an extra in the grandstands at the launch.

37

Director to the Second Power

Director George Romero's wife, Christine Forrest Romero, is the assistant director in a television studio in *Dawn of the Dead* (1978). Romero himself is the television director.

Mother's Day

Like so many of us, filmmakers have a soft spot for their mothers (or is it just primal fear?). You'll see mom slipping into quite a few movies.

I'LL HAVE WHAT SHE'S HAVING! *Director Rob Reiner gave his mom Estelle one of the best lines of the movie during the "fake orgasm" scene of* When Harry Met Sally... *(1989). (Photofest)*

38

One of the most delightful cameos was that played by Estelle Reiner, progenitor of director Rob, who says, "I'll have what she's having" during Meg Ryan's faked orgasm scene in the restaurant in *When Harry Met Sally...* (1989).

Martin Scorsese's mother Catherine appeared in many of his films, beginning in 1965 as the mother in his short subject *It's Not Just You, Murray!* She was the mother in *Who's That Knocking at My Door?* (1968), and played Rupert's (Robert De Niro) mom in *The King of Comedy* (1983). In *Mean Streets* (1973) she's the woman who helps Teresa (Amy Robinson) through an epileptic fit. She's the mother of Tommy (Joe Pesci) in the dinner scene in *GoodFellas* (1990). In *Cape Fear* (1991), she's a customer at a fruit stand, and in *Casino* (1995) she plays Piscano's (Vinny Vella) mother.

Scorsese provided work for his dad, Charles, too. Charles is with his real wife Catherine at the fruit stand in *Cape Fear*, and they are birthday guests in *Wise Guys* (1986). He plays Vinnie, who puts too many onions in the sauce in *GoodFellas* (1990). In *The Color of Money* (1986), he's the number one high roller, the first man at the bar in *The King of Comedy* (1983), and plays Charlie in *Raging Bull* (1980). He also makes cameo appearances in *The Age of Innocence* (1993) and *After Hours* (1985).

Jonathan Demme used his mother as one of the two old ladies in the resale shop in *Something Wild* (1986); the other was the mother of actor David Byrne. Pedro Almodovar's mother is in *Kika* (1993) as an interviewer in a TV program about writers.

The Kid Gets into the Act

It may be vanity, but it also may be an easy way to get one's offspring a SAG (Screen Actors Guild) card and a few residual checks for the college fund. You don't have to look too hard to find directors' kids in a movie.

Oliver Stone's son Sean is all over his dad's film projects. He's a boy at a grocery store in *U-Turn* (1997), young Donald Nixon in *Nixon* (1995), plays Kevin in *Natural Born Killers* (1994), is the young Jim Morrison in the accident scene in *The Doors* (1991), Jim Garrison's son Jasper in *JFK* (1991), young Jimmy in *Born on the*

Fourth of July (1989), Rudy Gekko in *Wall Street* (1987), and Boyle's (James Woods) baby in *Salvador* (1986).

An Inauspicious Beginning

Francis Ford Coppola's daughter Sofia is the infant in the christening scene in *The Godfather* (1972), while the elder Coppola's sister, Talia Shire, is Connie, the daughter who gets beaten up. A grown-up Sofia Coppola also reappeared, to scathing reviews, in *The Godfather Part III* (1990).

Get My Daughter on the Phone

Stanley Kubrick's daughter Vivian is Dr. Floyd's (William Sylvester) video-phone daughter in *2001: A Space Odyssey* (1968).

40

Delivering the Performance

John Boorman's son Charley plays Ed's (Jon Voight) son in his dad's *Deliverance* (1972). The younger Boorman went on to a starring role in another of his father's movies, *The Emerald Forest* (1985). He's the young Mordred in *Excalibur* (1981), a shot-down Luftwaffe Pilot in *Hope and Glory* (1987), the Green Man in *I Dreamt I Woke Up* (1991), a news photographer in *Beyond Rangoon* (1995), and a painter in *Two Nudes Bathing* (1995).

A Bad Boy's Good Beginning

Another director's son who went on to claim his own fame is Sean Penn, who was widely praised for his cameo during courtroom testimony in Leo Penn's *Judgment in Berlin* (1988).

Keeping Mom and Pop Off Welfare

Actors can help their relatives find work on film. When the studio couldn't get Spring Byington, who was busy with another picture, to play Ginger Rogers' mother in *The Major and the Minor* (1942), the role went to Lela Rogers, Ginger's real mother.

Watching Over the Kid

Mary Stuart Masterson's parents in *Gardens of Stone* (1987) are played by her real-life parents, Peter Masterson and Carlin Glynn.

41

Picture Perfect Parents

Sigourney Weaver's dad Pat, the legendary television executive, makes a silent cameo in *Half Moon Street* (1986). The photograph sitting near an answering machine is of Sigourney and her father. We're told that the actress who plays Weaver's daughter in *Aliens* (1986) is actually her mother.

Making the Phone Book Interesting

Dustin Hoffman slipped a reference to his family into *Rain Main* (1988). When he recites names from the phone book, two of them, Marsha and William Gottsegen, are his true-life in-laws.

Postal Routing

When a postal employee in the Norwegian film *Junk Mail* (1997) lists the people on his route, he mentions one Gong Li. This is the name of a distinguished Chinese actress, and star of Wayne Wang's *The Chinese Box* (1997).

Sister Act

John Travolta's sister Ellen is the pizza lady in *Saturday Night Fever* (1977), and their mom is the lady for whom Travolta buys paint. Ellen makes a return appearance as the waitress watching TV in *Grease* (1978).

Where No Daughter Has Gone Before

The Yeoman who holds Captain Kirk's malfunctioning captain's log in *Star Trek V: The Final Frontier* is William Shatner's daughter.

A Command(ment) Performance

Young Fraser Heston got an early start in the movies. He's the baby who floats up in the bullrushes in *The Ten Commandments* (1956), playing the infant Moses. Dad Charlton, of course, was the grown-up Moses.

If Daddy Could Do It

Like father, like daughter. Patricia Hitchcock can be seen in several of her father's films, including *Strangers on a Train* (1951), *Stage Fright* (1950), and *Psycho* (1960).

Soon-Yi Visits the Turkey Farm

Bad enough that Kevin Costner has starred in several notable turkeys (*did you really like* 1995's *Waterworld?*), we're a little concerned that the actress playing a mail carrier who has a crush on him in *The Postman* (1997) is his real-life daughter Annie. She also cameos with dad in *Dances with Wolves* (1990).

Scott's Spacey Kids

When Dallas (Tom Skerritt), Kane (John Hurt), and Lambert (Veronica Cartright) leave the ship in Ridley Scott's *Alien* (1979), the actors walking past the Nostromo's landing struts are actually children, used to make the ship look bigger. Two of the three actors are Scott's kids.

43

The Madsen Family Acts

Virginia Madsen stars in *Blue Tiger* (1994). Appearing in an uncredited cameo is her brother, Michael Madsen.

Seeing Double

Take notes. When the T-1000 killing machine (Robert Patrick) transforms into Sarah Conner in *Terminator 2: Judgment Day* (1991), what you're actually seeing is the twin (Leslie Hamilton Gearron) of Linda Hamilton, who plays Sarah Conner. And when the T-1000 transforms into Lewis, the security guard, what you're seeing is Don Stanton playing the guard, and *his* identical twin, Dan Stanton, playing the T-1000 transformed into the security guard. Capiche?

Sooner or Later, It All Comes Around

When Matt Damon praises *A People's History of the United States: 1492–1992* by Howard Zinn in *Good Will Hunting* (1997) you might think it's a book that impressed him when he was a college student. "That book will knock you on your ass," he says to Robin Williams, playing his therapist. But there's more to the tale. It turns out that Howard Zinn lived on the same street in Newton, MA, as Damon's family. The seventy-five-year-old Zinn told *Entertainment Weekly* the real reason his book is mentioned in Damon and Ben Affleck's script is that, "He's paying me back for all the cookies we gave him when he was a kid." Sales of the book zoomed after the movie came out.

PAYING HOMAGE

*I*t can be a tip of the hat or a thumb to the nose. Either way, it's an inside joke when a director, writer, or actor slips a cross-reference to his or her previous film(s) or to those of a friend into their movies.

Steven Spielberg and George Lucas are perhaps Hollywood's kings of this self-reference genre. There are all sorts of back-and-forth references to their movies hidden within the projects they've directed or produced. You'll find them peppered throughout this book. An example is the appearance of Lucas' R2D2 (the famed robot from the *Star Wars* trilogy) on the spacecraft that hovers over Devil's Mountain in Spielberg's *Close Encounters of the Third Kind* (1977). You may not be able to see it (or the shark from *Jaws* [1975] that's supposedly riding on the ship also) but we hear that it's there, a joke from the builders of the special effects props.

A SERIAL JOKE *Does the serial number of the airplane that rescues Indy (Harrison Ford) in* Raiders of the Lost Ark *(1981) look familiar? (Video screen photo, collection of the author)*

Spielberg's *Indiana Jones and the Temple of Doom* (1984) has a scene in Club Obi-Wan, a famous name from Lucas' *Star Wars* (1977), and in *Raiders of the Lost Ark* (1981). The airplane that rescues Indy (Harrison Ford) from the angry natives has OBI-CPO as its license numbers.

You have to wonder if every reference to a previous work is actually a joke, plug, or homage. Sometimes it's just a convenience. After all, it isn't easy to get rights clearances for film clips and trade names. If the director says sure, just use a clip from my other picture, it may just be a way to save a truckload of grief and legal fees. The assumption is that some are jokes, some aren't. Whatever.

Spotting for a Friend

When the title card appears at the beginning of "Jack Slater IV," the movie within a movie in *Last Action Hero* (1993), it says "A Franco Columbu Film." Columbu is a legendary body builder and friend of *Hero* star Arnold Schwarzenegger. This friend also appears in *Pumping Iron* (1977), *Conan the Barbarian* (1982), *The Terminator* (1984), and *The Running Man* (1987).

Paying Homage to the Schlockmeister

A cameo often can be a director's homage to a master of his genre, as in Roman Polanski's *Rosemary's Baby* (1968), where the legendary shock-schlock director William Castle is seen standing near a phone booth.

47

Homage to the King

A sly reference to a similar movie pops up in many films. One such is the naming of the ship that brings the dinosaur back to San Diego in *The Lost World: Jurassic Park* (1997) as the *Venture*, the same name of the ship that brought King Kong to America in the 1933 epic.

More and More Child's Play

When Brad Dourif is asked how he was able to get out of jail without being seen in *The Exorcist III: The Legion* (1990), he says, "It's child's play." He should know, he was the voice of Chucky, the evil doll in *Child's Play*, (1988), *Child's Play 2* (1990), and *Child's Play 3* (1991).

All the News That Fits

A newspaper seen in Joe Dante's *Explorers* (1985) says "Kingston Falls Mystery Still Unsolved." Kingston Falls was the town in Dante's *Gremlins* (1984).

Keep on Truckin'

The cyro-truck in James Cameron's *Terminator 2: Judgment Day* (1991) bears the name "Benthic Petroleum." That's also the name of the company in Cameron's *The Abyss* (1989).

The Director Was Burned

François Truffaut directed *Fahrenheit 451* (1966), the title being a reference to the temperature at which paper burns. Among the publications burned by the firemen is *Cahiers du Cinema*, the film magazine for which Truffaut wrote before becoming a filmmaker. On the cover is a shot from *A Bout de Soufflé* (aka *Breathless*) (1959), a movie written by Truffaut.

A Few Good Plugs

While Danny (Tom Cruise) watches a ball game in *A Few Good Men* (1992), two copies of Stephen King's novel, *Misery*, are seen near his typewriter. Rob Reiner directed both *A Few Good Men* and *Misery* (1990), the film made from King's novel.

Let's Sell a Few Videos

The front window of a video store in *The Fisher King* (1991) displays a poster of *The Adventures of Baron*

Munchausen (1989), both directed by Terry Gilliam. A poster for Gilliam's *Brazil* (1985) is on a wall of the store.

Trailer Talk

Before the "Misbehavors" turn to the sports channel in Robert Rodriguez' segment of *Four Rooms* (1995) they're watching a short film by... Robert Rodriguez.

Heavenly Plugs

Set decorators on Peter Jackson's *The Frighteners* (1996) placed a copy of Jackson's *Heavenly Creatures* (1994) next to the TV set while Lucy (Trini Alvarado) is watching the video about Johnny Bartlett (Jake Busey).

49

There's No Escaping It

Harry Saltzman and Albert Broccoli produced *From Russia with Love* (1963), the second of the James Bond spy film series. Notice that when Krilencu (Fred Haggerty) tries to escape through a secret window in a billboard, it's advertising *Call Me Bwana* (1963), also produced by Saltzman and Broccoli.

Same Job, Different Title

The letter telling Nora (Brooke Adams) about Trudi's (Ione Skye) absences from school in *Gas Food Lodging* (1992) gives the name of the school principal as Allison Anders. Anders was the director of the film; her job, we suppose, could be compared to that of a school principal.

Coen Coming Attractions

Factory workers in Joel and Ethan Coen's *Raising Arizona* (1987) are wearing uniforms that say "Hudsucker Industries," thus acting as a precursor to the Coen Brothers' *The Hudsucker Proxy* (1994). Also in *The Hudsucker Proxy* the chief (Trey Williams) says, "Yeah, and if a frog had wings it wouldn't bump its ass a'hoppin'," just as Nathan Arizona did in the previous film, thus providing a *quid pro quo* between the films.

Return of the Promo

Richard Marquand hyped his *Return of the Jedi* (1983) with a poster in the bedroom of David (Brandon Call) and Jenny (Christina Hutter) Barnes when he directed *Jagged Edge* (1985).

The Reitman Stuff

Dominic (played by youngsters Joseph Cousins and his brother Christian) has *Ghostbusters* sheets on his bed in Ivan Reitman's *Kindergarten Cop* (1990). Guess who directed *Ghostbusters* (1984)?

He's Back

As the star of *Last Action Hero* (1993), Arnold Schwarzenegger was able to get a tribute to his directorial debut in the 1992 TV movie *Christmas in Connecticut* by making it very visible in a video store.

Lethal Plug

The movie that Darian (Danielle Harris) is watching on TV in *The Last Boy Scout* (1991) is *Lethal Weapon* (1987). Shane Black wrote both films.

Lethal Plug: The Sequel

While the Murtagh family waits for the commercial in *Lethal Weapon 2* (1989), they watch an episode of TV's long-running *Tales from the Crypt* (1994–) starring Mary Ellen Trainer, who plays the police psychiatrist in *LW2*.

The Mighty Oz

Moviemaker Frank Oz makes sure you know who helmed *Little Shop of Horrors* (1986). When the "Chooz" sign blinks, the first three letters go out, leaving it to read "oz."

51

The Perfect Ten

Number ten on the Duck's rival team in *The Mighty Ducks* (1992) is named Herek, as in the director, Stephen Herek.

When Harry Met Misery

Harry (Billy Crystal) reads Stephen King's novel *Misery* in *When Harry Met Sally...* (1989). *Misery* (1990) would be Rob Reiner's next directorial effort.

When Misery Met Sally

A video of *When Harry Met Sally...* (1989) can be seen in the general store in *Misery* (1990).

CREATING MISERY *Director Rob Reiner made several cross-references to his production of* Misery *(1990) in both earlier and later directorial efforts. Look for them in* When Harry Met Sally... *(1989) and* A Few Good Men *(1992). (The Blackburn Archive)*

52

The Playboy Play

You never know what's a joke and what isn't in *Naked Gun 33 $^{1}/_{3}$: The Final Insult* (1994). But we assume there's some meaning in showing the cover of the *Playboy* magazine that Papschmir (Raye Birk) is reading in the Lear jet which features the buxom Anna Nicole Smith. Smith plays Tanya Peters in the film.

This Is a Sure Thing

Rob Reiner continues his homage to previous works in *The Sure Thing* (1985). A poster for his *This Is Spinal*

Tap (1984) can be seen in Gib's (John Cusack) college dorm room.

So That's What He Thinks of the Old Home Town

The oil tanker struck by the ship in *Speed 2: Cruise Control* (1997) is *The Eindhoven*. Eindhoven is director Jan de Bont's hometown.

A Swinging Tribute

The guys in *Swingers* (1996) know that George Lucas is, in their terms, "the money," as acknowledged in their use of the Lucas trademark "THX 1138" on the license plate of Trent's (Vince Vaughn) car.

Back to the Antique Store

53

In *Back to the Future Part II* (1989), when Marty (Michael J. Fox) shows up in the year 2015, a Roger Rabbit doll is for sale in an antique store. Robert Zemeckis directed both *BTTF Part II* and *Who Framed Roger Rabbit* (1988). Producer Steven Spielberg is honored with a *Jaws* (1975) Nintendo game in the same window display.

Relatively Speaking

Lauren Bacall mentions "That old man in *The African Queen* (1951)" in *How to Marry a Millionaire* (1953). That old man was, of course, her husband Humphrey Bogart. In the same movie, Betty Grable doesn't recognize a Harry James recording. James was her husband at the time.

Indecent Plug

In *Indecent Proposal* (1993), Diana (Demi Moore) is reading John Grisham's novel *The Firm* (1991), which would be Paramount's next 1993 hit. The secretary in the real estate office where she works is reading the book *Backlash* (1992), which criticizes director Adrian Lyne's portrayal of women in his films.

Dead-já Vu

Goldie Hawn drinks the magic potion on October 25, 1985, in Robert Zemeckis' *Death Becomes Her* (1992). That's the present date in *Back to the Future* (1985), also directed by Zemeckis.

54

Perfect Bull

When Butch (Kevin Costner) and Phillip (T. J. Lowther) visit a department store in *A Perfect World* (1993) you can see a poster for *Bull Durham* (1988), which also starred Costner.

He Might Even Be an Actor, for All We Know

Bruce Willis gets a gentle jibe in *Die Hard* (1988), when Reginald Vel Johnson tells Paul Gleason the voice he hears on the radio may be a cop. Gleason says, "He might be a bartender for all we know." Willis, star of the film, was a bartender before getting his big break in the TV detective series *Moonlighting* (1985–89).

She Oughta Know

The teacher praising the work of Sir Laurence Olivier in *Last Action Hero* (1993) knows of whom she speaks. Joan Plowright, playing the teacher, was married to Olivier.

Cubed Promo

The boom box that rapper Ice Cube, playing Danny in *Anaconda* (1997), has is playing a tune by, guess who, Ice Cube.

Recycled Names

The airplane that explodes in Jan de Bont's *Speed* (1994) bears the name *Pacific Courier*, which was also the name on the terrorist van in *Die Hard* (1988). Jan de Bont was cinematographer of the latter film.

55

Sucking Up to the Director

In *Scream* (1996), when Casey (Drew Barrymore) complains that all of the sequels to *Nightmare on Elm Street* (1984) sucked, it might just be a suck-up to *Scream* director Wes Craven. Craven directed the original *Nightmare*, but directed none of its sequels.

Remembrance of Things Past

Take note: Both Bruce Willis and Samuel Jackson starred in *Pulp Fiction* (1994). At one point in *Die Hard with a Vengeance* (1995), Willis tells Jackson, "I was just getting used to my day job, smoking cigarettes and watching *Captain Kangaroo*." The phrase was a line from

"Flowers on the Wall" by the Statler brothers, from the soundtrack of *Pulp Fiction*.

Daniel Day of Remembrance

Daniel Day-Lewis starred in *The Last of the Mohicans* (1992), an event that is remembered in *The Age of Innocence* (1993) with a painting of a scene from his previous film.

Tanking the Homage

John Carpenter tips the hat (or lifts a seat) to fellow film maven George Lucas in his *Dark Star* (1974). A piece of debris seen after the ship blows up is a THX 1138 Toilet Tank. In the same film, he gives his producer the kind of mention you really don't want. For a brief moment, a computer screen says "Fuck You, Harris." Jack H. Harris co-produced and distributed the movie.

56

Starting the Ball Rolling

Robert Altman, who directed the landmark comedy *M*A*S*H* (1970), used a poster for the film progenitor of the long-running TV series (1972–83) in Suzanne's (Shelley Duvall) apartment in his *Brewster McCloud* (1970). Also in *Brewster*, check out Margaret Hamilton's ruby slippers, a witchy reference to another film (surely you know the one) in which she starred.

Sounds Familiar

When Dennis (John Stockwell) pulls a book off the library shelf just before asking Leigh (Alexandra Paul) out in *Christine* (1983), it's a familiar Stephen King title: *Christine* (1983).

Nightmarish and Evil Reciprocity

A torn poster for *The Hills Have Eyes* (1977) in *The Evil Dead* (1983) is director Sam Raimi's tribute to friend Wes Craven, who directed *Hills*. Then, in Craven's *Nightmare on Elm Street* (1984) a scene from Raimi's *The Evil Dead* can be seen on a television screen. Are you still with us? Next, in Raimi's *Evil Dead II: Dead by Dawn* (1987), one of Freddy Krueger's gloves from Craven's *Nightmare* can be seen hanging near some steps.

A Numerical Tribute

Dan Ackroyd, playing John Burns, wears the prison number, 74-74-505-B, in *The Couch Trip* (1988). The number is the same as that worn by Jake Blues (John Belushi) in *The Blues Brothers* (1980), in which Ackroyd co-starred.

Son of a Numerical Tribute

The number on Roman's prison uniform in Kenneth Branagh's *Dead Again* (1991) is 25101415, representing 25 October 1415, a significant date for the director. Branagh's previous film was *Henry V* (1989), in which England's King Henry fought the Battle of Agincourt on that date. Another date reference in the thriller is December 10 in a newspaper clipping sequence; that's actor/director Branagh's birthday.

KENNETH'S BATTLES
Kenneth Branagh's prison number in Dead Again *(1991) is the date of the Battle of Agincourt (25 October 1415), a climactic moment in his previous film,* Henry V *(1989).*
(Photofest)

I, Stutterer

Derek Jacobi stutters in *Dead Again* (1991), recalling the character he played, the Roman Emperor Claudius, in the landmark TV mini-series *I, Claudius* (1977).

Family Videos

A poster for *Frauds* (1993) shows up in a video store in *The Adventures of Priscilla, Queen of the Desert* (1994). Both films were directed by Stephan Elliott, and both starred Hugo Weaving.

Underground Honors

"Harry Lime Lives" is the graffiti on a sewer wall in *Alligator* (1980), directed by Lewis Teague. In *The Third*

Man (1949), Harry Lime, one of Orson Welles' most memorable screen roles, was killed in a sewer. Also in *Alligator*, on a blackboard in the background of a press conference is the name of several victims, including "Edward Norton," the memorable sewer worker character played by Art Carney in TV's *The Honeymooners* between 1951 and 1971.

Sign of Progress

The automobile dealership in *Back to the Future Part III* (1990) is Statler Toyota. In the first of the series, *Back to the Future* (1985), the horse dealer was named Statler.

A Painful Tribute

When Joe Pesci is pushed into a hole in the desert in *Casino* (1995), it was a painful and real-life case of déjà-vu. He broke the same rib he broke during a scene in *Raging Bull* (1980).

Recalling the "Chill"

A street urchin character in Lawrence Kasdan's *Grand Canyon* (1991) mentions Beaufort, South Carolina, the setting for Kasdan's earlier movie, *The Big Chill* (1983).

Singing His Song

Lawrence Kasdan wrote the script for Steven Spielberg's *Raiders of the Lost Ark* (1981). Perhaps that's why Harold (Kevin Kline), in Kasdan's *The Big Chill* (1983), hums the theme from *Raiders* as he fights off the marauding bat.

BACK AGAIN *Gregory Peck, who starred as Sam Bowden in the 1962 version of* Cape Fear, *makes a cameo appearance as a lawyer defending Cady in Martin Scorsese's 1991 version. Robert Mitchum, who was the villain Max Cady in the earlier version, is the town sheriff in 1991. (JC Archives)*

Pod People Redux

The pod that Dr. Catheter (Christopher Lee) carries in *Gremlins 2: The New Batch* (1990) might look familiar; it's from *Invasion of the Body Snatchers* (1956).

A Painful Precursor

In *Peggy Sue Got Married* (1986), Nicolas Cage begs Kathleen Turner to marry him, saying he doesn't know what the future might bring; he might even lose an arm. Guess what? In *Moonstruck* (1987) he plays a character with a hand and part of his arm missing!

Twice-Told Tales

When Bunny (Susan Fallender) tells a joke in *Trading Places* (1983), the punch line is, "and she stepped on the ball." If it sounds familiar, it's the punch line of the awful joke that Joanna Barnes, as Gloria Upson, tells in *Auntie Mame* (1958).

Scorsese's Recycled Actors

Martin Scorsese peppered his remake of *Cape Fear* (1991) with cast members of the 1962 version of the same film. Gregory Peck, who starred as Sam Bowden in the earlier film, plays lawyer Lee Heller in the update. Robert Mitchum was Max Cady in the 1962 version, and Lieutenant Elgart in the 1991 edition. Martin Balsam was Mark Dutton in 1962, and the judge in 1991.

61

Selling the Soundtrack

A record store in Stanley Kubrick's *A Clockwork Orange* (1971) is selling the soundtrack album for *2001: A Space Odyssey* (1968), also helmed by Kubrick.

Back and Forward to the Future

Child actors in *Shoot the Moon* (1982) sing music from *Fame* (1980), both of which were directed by Alan Parker. On a wall there's a poster for Parker's rock-musical drama *Pink Floyd: The Wall* (1982), a filmed version of their 1979 album, which was not released until five months later.

A Commitment to Self-Promotion *In this video-store scene in Alan Parker's* The Commitments *(1991), all of the videos in the background are of Alan Parker movies. (Photofest)*

Alan Parker Redux

One of the audition songs used in Alan Parker's *The Commitments* (1991) is from his film *Fame* (1980). In *The Commitments*, Jimmy is asked if he brought *Mississippi Burning* (1988) with him on the bus. Do we have to tell you who directed *Mississippi Burning*?

Que Sera, Sera

Doris Day goes to see a Doris Day film in *Caprice* (1967).

Probably Not the Centerfold

A character in Oliver Stone's *Talk Radio* (1988) reads a copy of *Playboy*. The issue is the one that carries an interview with Stone.

He Brought It from Home

Mark Poll designed the sets for both *Lethal Weapon 3* (1992) and *Demolition Man* (1993). Is that why there's a poster for *LW3* in Lenina Huxley's office in the latter film?

Mommie Dearest

Check out the last scene of *Psycho* (1960) and you'll see that Alfred Hitchcock copied the shot from the famous painting, *Whistler's Mother*.

Invasion of the Taxi Driver

Legendary filmmaker Don Siegel, who directed the original *Invasion of the Body Snatchers* (1956), shows up in Philip Kaufman's 1978 remake as a taxi driver. Kevin McCarthy, who starred as Dr. Miles J. Binnell in the 1956 film, cameos as a running man in the remake.

63

Shaking with Laughter

If you live in Southern California, or even if you don't and watch the news from the Shaky State, you'll often see Dr. Kate Hutton of Caltech on TV explaining the magnitude of the *quake de jour*. That's why L. A. theatres resounded with hearty laughter when Laurie Latham, playing a seismologist, showed up in *Volcano* (1997) with Hutton's trademark wire-rim glasses and short, salt-and-pepper hairdo.

The Recycled Spell

The character Willow (Warwick Davis), in the 1988 film of the same name, uses the same incantation as Merlin in *Excalibur* (1981).

Donner Blitzing

Richard Donner directed *X-15* (1961), and a poster hyping it appears in his *Radio Flyer* (1992).

Planning for the Future

The kids watch *The Thing from Another World* (1951) on TV in John Carpenter's *Halloween* (1978). Carpenter would later remake the film in 1982 as *The Thing*.

Robbie, Call Home

Robby the Robot from *Forbidden Planet* (1956) makes a couple of appearances in *Gremlins* (1985). In one scene, he's talking in a phone booth and wearing a hat. His dialogue comes from *Forbidden Planet* also, as it is the end of the conversation with the cook of the C-57-D where Earl Holliman, as Cookie, is trying to get Robby to distill some booze.

Now They Get Their Credit

Extra footage was added when *Superman* (1978) played on television. Among the additions were uncredited cameos of Lois Lane's parents on the train. The roles are played by two stars of the old Superman movie serials: Kirk Alyn, who played Superman, and Noel Neill, who played Lois Lane, both in the serials and with George Reeves in the 1950s TV series.

Now You See It, Now You Don't

While the father is talking on the phone at the inventor's convention in *Gremlins* (1984), you can see the elaborate time-travel device from *The Time Machine* (1960) spinning up in the background. The scene cuts away, and when it comes back there's only a wisp of smoke where the machine used to be, just like in the original movie.

Music to the Boss' Ears

There's an old saying about company loyalty: "Whose bread I eat, his song I sing." Composer Rick Wakeman knew whereupon his bread was buttered in *Crimes of Passion* (1984). The film was released by New World Pictures. Wakeman's soundtrack is based on Antonin Dvorak's Ninth Symphony, known as the "New World Symphony."

65

Zapping It

Frank Zappa's *Two Hundred Motels* (1971) was filmed in the same studio as *2001: A Space Odyssey* (1968). You can see the famed black monolith from Stanley Kubrick's landmark film in one scene.

The Conrad Connection

The ship *Nostromo* in *Alien* (1979) gets its name from a Joseph Conrad novel (1904) of the same name. When

Ripley (Sigourney Weaver) escapes, she's on a shuttle named the *Narcissus*, again after a Conrad work, *The Nigger of the Narcissus* (1897).

Working Their Way to Heaven

When Barbara (Geena Davis) and Adam (Alec Baldwin) are in their caseworker's office in *Beetlejuice* (1988), through the blinds you can see Elwood (Dan Aykroyd) and Jake (John Belushi) Blues from *The Blues Brothers* (1980).

The Film within the Film

Rachel (Whitney Houston) and Frank (Kevin Costner) go to see Akira Kurosawa's *Yojimbo* (1961) in *The Bodyguard* (1992). *Yojimbo* was released in America as *The Bodyguard*.

TALISMANS AND TRADEMARKS

*W*hether it's for luck, for friendship, or just as a whim, many directors stamp personal trademarks onto their films. Some are shooting styles, often so subtle and obscure that only a serious film buff can locate them. Brian de Palma often uses a 360-degree panoramic shot to make a point. Orson Welles was known for his extremely long scenes without edit cuts. Jim Cameron does highly-crafted dissolves.

Taking a trademark to a new level is the *Indiana Jones* trilogy. Notice in the beginning of *Raiders of the Lost Ark* (1981) the Paramount logo fades into the silhouette of an identically shaped mountain. In *Indiana Jones and the Temple of Doom* (1984), the shape of the Paramount logo is on a gong. In *Indiana Jones and the Last Crusade* (1989) it's a similarly shaped rock in Utah.

TAGGING HIS WORK *The license plate on the roadster in* American Graffiti *(1973) is the name of George Lucas' first feature film,* THX 1138 *(1971). (Video screen photo, collection of the author)*

There are director trademarks and there are actor trademarks. Watch how Val Kilmer flips two coins across his knuckles in *Real Genius* (1985). Then watch him do it with a pen in *Top Gun* (1986), a coin again in *The Doors* (1991), and a poker chip in *Tombstone* (1993).

In fact, the coin roll goes all the way back to George Raft, who built his own inside joke on it. When he sees a young hood flipping a coin in *Some Like It Hot* (1959), he says, "Where did you pick up that cheap trick?" It's a piece of business Raft himself made famous in *Scarface* (1932), and the actor to whom he directs the line is Edward G. Robinson Jr., son of his old screen rival.

Lucas' THX 1138

As noted variously in this book, George Lucas and other directors who admire his work often use THX 1138 or some variation of it in their screen work. It's the title of Lucas' first feature film as well as the name of the character played by Robert Duvall, and he uses it as "THX 138" on the license plate of John Milner's roadster in *American Graffiti* (1973). In *Star Wars* (1977), Han Solo (Harrison Ford) and Luke Skywalker (Mark Hamill) liberate Chewbacca from Cell 1138. One reference also says that the THX came from "Tomlinson Holman's eXperiment," Holman being the inventor of the famous sound system and audio engineer for many of Lucas' films.

69

Tarantino's Big Kahuna

Quentin Tarantino puts a special signature on his work with a couple of props. Big Kahuna Burgers and Red Apple cigarettes first showed up in *True Romance* (1993), which was written by Tarantino.

In *Pulp Fiction* (1994), Samuel L. Jackson touts Big Kahuna burgers and both Bruce Willis and Uma Thurman smoke Red Apple cigarettes. In *From Dusk till Dawn* (1996) George Clooney carries a Big Kahuna burger bag, and you can spot a pack of Red Apples in his car. In *Four Rooms* (1995) Red Apples smokes are near the switchboard.

"It's a signature thing," graphic designer Jerry Martinez told *Entertainment Weekly*, "It's Quentin's way

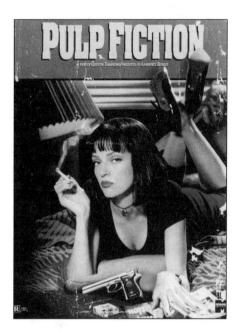

TARENTINO'S
SMOKING TRADEMARK
*Characters in
Quentin
Tarentino's films
almost always
smoke Red Apple
cigarettes, as does
Uma Thurman in
this poster from*
Pulp Fiction
*(1994). (The
Blackburn Archive)*

of saying all these different characters share the same universe."

Taking it to a new level, even though Tarantino didn't direct *Romy and Michelle's High School Reunion* (1997) (David Mirkin did), the props show up there, also. This time it's partly an in-joke, partly a convenience. One of the film's stars, Mira Sorvino, was then Tarantino's main squeeze. The picture's production designer, a friend of Martinez, didn't want to go through the laborious process of getting clearances for the use of actual trademarked products. Look for the Big Kahuna burger bag when Sorvino and costar Lisa Kudrow are pigging out, and there's an ad for Red Apple cigarettes on the building next to their apartment.

Fred's Fanfare

In several of their musicals, when Fred Astaire and Ginger Rogers dance, the number starts with a bugle call. The gag originated in *The Gay Divorcee* (1934) with some clowning around on the set during rehearsals. It made it into the film, and you'll hear it again in *Roberta* (1935), *Follow the Fleet* (1936), and when he starred with Rita Hayworth in *You'll Never Get Rich* (1941).

Sam and Shemp

Director Sam Raimi pays homage to The Three Stooges in many of his movies. In *Army of Darkness* (1993) skeletons perform a Stooges routine. In *Crimewave* (1985), among the slapstick bits is a scene of bowling balls rolling off a shelf onto a man's head, just as it happened in a Stooges routine. *Darkman* (1990) and *The Evil Dead* (1983) also have Stooges references.

A Raimi movie often has a "fake Shemp." In his formative years, he noticed that after the death of Shemp Howard, Columbia didn't want to reshoot the uncompleted films, nor did they want to let Moe Howard and Larry Fine out of their contracts. So, they used a double for Shemp, and they turned his face away from the camera. Raimi adopted this technique when he needed bit players for his films, often actors doing bigger roles elsewhere. Later it came to be a term for friends playing bit roles. Among his "fake Shemps" are Don and Charlie Campbell, father and brother of Bruce (see below). You'll also see Raimi's brothers, Ivan and Ted, in many of his films.

The Campbell Gambit

Actor Bruce Campbell is another Raimi trademark. He was a high-school buddy of Raimi's back in Michigan, where they made 8mm movies together. You'll see him in most Raimi movies, and if he's not there it's either because his part was cut or the studio wouldn't let Raimi cast his buddy. That's what happened in *Crimewave* (1985), and when Embassy Pictures, the studio that released it, collapsed, Raimi was quoted as saying, "God has seen fit to dismember them and sow salt where their offices once were so nothing would grow." Now, that's vengeance!

72

The Kubrick Number

For some unexplained reason, Stanley Kubrick trademarks many of his films with the number 114. In *2001: A Space Odyssey* (1968) the Jupiter Explorer's serial number is CRM-114. In *A Clockwork Orange* (1971), Alex (Malcolm McDowell) is given Serum 114 while undergoing the Ludovico treatment. In *Dr. Strangelove or: How I Learned to Stop Worrying and Love the Bomb* (1964) it is the message decoder, identified as the CRM-114 on the B-52. Robert Zemeckis acknowledges Kubrick by naming the device into which Marty (Michael J. Fox) plugs his guitar in Doc's (Christopher Lloyd) lab CRM-114 in *Back to the Future* (1985). In a mixed metaphor, both George Lucas and Kubrick are saluted with the license plate on a police car in the Japanese film *Riding Bean* (1989), which reads THX-114B.

Coen Casting

The Coen Brothers, Ethan and Joel, trademark several of their films with recurring actors. John Turturro is a favorite. He shows up in *Miller's Crossing* (1990), *Barton Fink* (1991), and *The Big Lebowski* (1998). John Goodman is another Coen regular, appearing in *The Big Lebowski*, *Barton Fink*, *The Hudsucker Proxy* (1994), and *Raising Arizona* (1987).

73

Gordon's Artistic Charm

Michael Gordon, who directed *For Love or Money* (1963) had a very special good luck charm. He always included a painting by his favorite artist, Edgar O. Kiechle. As he placed one on the wall behind Kirk Douglas, the actor said, "I've worked with a lot of tough directors, but he's the first one who insisted on holding something over an actor's head."

Harlin's Patriotism

Finnish director Renny Harlin is so enthusiastic about including references to his home country that in one film, *Cutthroat Island* (1995) the Finnish flag he placed in a shop window creates an anachronism; it wasn't in use at the time in which the swashbuckler was set. In *The Long Kiss Goodnight* (1996) graffiti that reads "Hell Sink" (Helsinki) is on a pay phone, and characters drink Finlandia vodka. In *Cliffhanger* (1993), one of the parachutes resembles the Finnish flag. In *Die Hard 2: Die Harder* (1990), snippets of Finnish composer Jean Sibelius' hymn "Finlandia" are heard throughout the action flick.

SEE YOU NEXT WEDNESDAY: THE LANDIS GAMBITS

*J*ohn Landis occupies a special place in the pantheon of directors who trademark their screen works, sometimes subtly, sometimes not. His fans search for the best-known Landis hallmark, the use of the phrase "See You Next Wednesday" whenever a new film is released.

Landis was quoted in the *Los Angeles Times* as saying that the phrase was the title of his first screenplay. "I keep including references to it because, basically, I've been cannibalizing it for years."

Landis' line also has other derivations in film history. The *Times*' Michael London pointed out it was often the tag line on a trailer back in the days when movies opened regularly on Wednesdays, and it was also a line of dialog between the astronaut and his parents in Stanley Kubrick's *2001: A Space Odyssey* (1968).

Whatever its origins, look for Landis' inventive use of the trademark phrase in these films:

Schlock (1971): on a poster in a theatre lobby, and promoted with a trailer which says, "First, *Birth of a Nation*. Then, *Gone with the Wind* . . . *2001: A Space Odyssey* . . . *See You Next Wednesday* . . . and now *Schlock*"

The Kentucky Fried Movie (1977): the title of the Feel-A-Rama movie

The Blues Brothers (1980): A cop hides behind a billboard advertising a film, *See You Next Wednesday*, "Coming Soon to a Theatre Near You."

An American Werewolf in London (1981): It's the title for the porno film that's showing when David (David Naughton) meets the zombies. A poster for it shows up in the London Underground.

Trading Places (1983): It appears on a poster in the subway.

Twilight Zone: The Movie (1983): It is spoken in German when Bill (Vic Morrow) is being shot at on the building.

Spies Like Us (1985): It is seen on a recruiting poster behind the desk of the army commander at the training post.

SEE YA... *It's a John Landis trademark: the phrase "See You Next Wednesday" displayed in various ways in his movies. This one's from* The Blues Brothers *(1980). (Video screen photo, collection of the author)*

Into the Night (1985): It shows up on two posters in the office where Ed (Jeff Goldblum) and Diana (Michelle Pfieffer) make a phone call.

Coming to America (1988): Again, the phrase appears on a bogus subway movie poster, claiming to star Jamie Lee Curtis. Curtis actually appeared in Landis' 1983 film, *Trading Places*. In this latter film, there was also a poster with this phrase seen in the apartment of Ophelia, the role that Curtis played in that film.

Innocent Blood (1992): The saying is advertised on a marquee across the street from the Melody Lounge dance hall.

The Stupids (1996): It is on the back of a bus to which the kids chain their bikes.

A Cast of Directors

Another John Landis trademark is to include his fellow filmmakers in small roles in his films. Here's your challenge: See if you can find these famous directors:

The Blues Brothers (1980): Steven Spielberg and Frank Oz

Trading Places (1983): Frank Oz is the corrupt cop.

78

Into the Night (1985): Jack Arnold, David Cronenberg, Jonathan Demme, Amy Heckerling, Jim Henson, Colin Huggins, Lawrence Kasdan, John Landis, Jonathan Lynn, Paul Mazursky, Daniel Petrie, Don Siegel, and Roger Vadim

Spies Like Us (1985): Michael Apted, Martin Brest, Joel Coen, Larry Cohen, Constantin Costa-Gravas, Terry Gilliam, Frank Oz, Sam Raimi, special effects genius Ray Harryhausen, along with cinematographer Robert Paynter, and visual effects artist Derek Meddings

Amazon Women on the Moon (1987): Russ Meyer, composer Ira Newborn, and *Famous Monsters of Filmland* editor Forrest J. Ackerman

Coming to America (1988) Jim Abrahams is the face on the cutting room floor.

Oscar (1991): Joe Dante is the face on the cutting room floor.

Innocent Blood (1992): Dario Argento, Frank Oz, Sam Raimi, Michael Ritchie, *Famous Monsters of Filmland* editor Forrest J. Ackerman, and make-up artist Tom Savini

Beverly Hills Cop III (1994): Martha Coolidge, Joe Dante, Arthur Hiller, George Lucas, Peter Medak, George Schaefer, Barbet Schroeder, and John Singleton, as well as special effects genius Ray Harryhausen

The Stupids (1996): Gurindia Chada, Constantin Costa-Gravas, David Cronenberg, Atom Egoyan, Mick Garris, Norman Jewison, Gillo Pontecarvo, and Robert Wise

Blues Brothers 2000 (1998): The only one we picked out was Frank Oz. There are probably more.

We're sure there are more. It's up to you. Let the searching begin.

The Ipanema Gambit

Continuing with the string of John Landis trademarks, there's another. You'll hear the song "Ipanema" in several Landis movies, including *Into the Night* (1985) where it's the music used during the strip scene. In *The Blues Brothers* (1980) you can hear it in an elevator.

Other directors have picked up on the "Ipanema" theme. It's the background music when T. S. (Jeremy London) and Hamilton (Ben Affleck) are waiting for an elevator in Kevin Smith's *Mallrats* (1995), and one of the characters hums it in the forgettable *Deep Rising* (1998).

And Finally...

Putting a ribbon on the Landis quirkography, the ubiquitous director also has a habit of showing up in his films and those of others. Sylvester Stallone runs over him in Paul Bartel's *Death Race 2000* (1975). Working as a young production assistant in *Kelly's Heroes* (1970), Landis couldn't find enough extras who would play sacrilegious nuns, so he put on one of the habits himself. He's the tallest nun. He bursts into flame in Tobe Hooper's *Spontaneous Combustion* (1990). In *Sleepwalkers* (1992) he plays a lab technician who tells Stephen King to "go talk to someone in charge. I'm busy" as he picks gore off a corpse. Here's a partial list:

80

Vampirella (1996): astronaut #1

Silenzio dei proscuitti II (aka *The Silence of the Hams*) (1994): FBI Agent

Venice/Venice (1992): himself

Body Chemistry 2: Voice of a Stranger (1991): Dr. Edwards

Darkman (1990): physician hidden behind surgical scrubs

Spontaneous Combustion (1990): radio technician

Into the Night (1985): one of the Arabs chasing Jeff Goldblum

The Muppets Take Manhattan (1984): the cruel manager

An American Werewolf in London (1981): man being smashed into a window

The Blues Brothers (1980): Trooper La Fong

1941 (1979): Mizerany

The Kentucky Fried Movie (1977): TV technician fighting with a gorilla

Death Race 2000 (1975): mechanic

Battle for the Planet of the Apes (1973): Jake's friend

Schlock (1971): the Schlockthropolus (in a gorilla suit, playing a lovesick King Kong)

WHERE'S ALFRED?

*T*he cinematic equivalent of artist Martin Handford's intricately illustrated *Where's Waldo?* puzzle books is the search for Alfred Hitchcock's cameo appearances in most of his films. For decades, fans of the master of suspense have made great sport of locating the portly director as he makes his trademark cameo appearances.

There is a common misconception that he appeared in all of his films. However, of his fifty-four-film *oeuvre*, Hitchcock shows up in only thirty-nine (unless you can find him in some that the experts have missed!). Oddly enough, only once did he carry the gimmick over to his long-running television show, even though he personally introduced the episodes. In the "Dip in the Pool" installment of *Alfred Hitchcock Presents* (1955–65), he shows up on the cover of a magazine.

It is said that the cameos began early in his career when he needed more extras, but couldn't afford them. The easiest thing was to appear in the scenes himself. Interestingly, even though his persona was somewhat foreboding, quite often he appears in humorous and self-deprecating cameos.

The gimmick began to take off in *Blackmail* (1929), a film that was his and England's first talking picture, even though it was originally shot as a silent. Hitchcock shows up sitting in a subway car reading a book. A small boy annoys him, and he swats at the kid with the book.

Perhaps the most original was in *Lifeboat* (1944). There was no way the pudgy director could slip into the boat with Tallulah Bankhead and the rest of the cast out in the middle of the ocean. So, playing on his ample physique, he shows up in an advertisement for men's corsets, the "Reduco Obesity Slayer," in a newspaper held by William Bendix. The before and after shots in the ad are both Hitchcock, as he had recently gone on a crash diet.

Lifeboat also produced one of the most enduring Hitchcock anecdotes. After cast members complained the uninhibited Tallulah Bankhead wasn't wearing undies and they were seeing a bit too much of her as she climbed in and out of the soundstage boat, he is report-ed to have said, "I don't know whether this is a matter for the costume department or the hairdresser."

Hitchcock's cameos are all silent, except for his nar-ration of the prologue in *The Wrong Man* (1957). Oddly,

ALFRED SLIMS DOWN *Hitchcock couldn't crawl into the boat with the cast of* Lifeboat *(1944), so he shows up in a newspaper ad. Both pictures are of Hitchcock, before and after a crash diet.* (Photofest)

85

the only recurring theme seems to be Hitch's carrying of a stringed instrument (a cello, a violin, and a double bass) in three of the cameos.

His last onscreen appearance carried a heavy portent for his future. In *Family Plot* (1976), Hitchcock's fifty-fourth and final film, he's seen in silhouette obtaining two death certificates from the registrar's office. Hitchcock died in 1980.

Lucky you. We've done the hard work and prepared a list of Hitchcock cameos in most of his films. Now it's up to you to find him.

The Hitchcock Cameos

The Lodger (1926): sitting at a desk in the newsroom scene, and in a crowd scene near the end of the film

Easy Virtue (1927): walks past a tennis court carrying a walking stick

Blackmail (1929): sitting in a subway car, reading a newspaper which he uses to swat at a small boy who annoys him

Murder (1930): walks past the house where the homicide was committed

The 39 Steps (1935): tossing litter as Robert Donat and Lucie Mannheim run from the theatre

Sabotage (1936): buying a ticket at the box office

Young and Innocent (1937): the bumbling photographer outside the courthouse

The Lady Vanishes (1938): at Victoria Station, wearing a black coat and smoking a cigarette

Jamaica Inn (1939): a costume appearance, wearing a waistcoat and top hat

Foreign Correspondent (1940): after Joel McCrea leaves his hotel, Hitchcock walks past reading a newspaper

Rebecca (1940): waiting outside a phone booth for George Sanders to finish using it

Mr. and Mrs. Smith (1941): walks past Robert Montgomery, about halfway through the movie

87

ALFRED AND THE KIDS *In one of Alfred Hitchcock's delightful on-screen cameos, a kid harasses him on a subway in* Blackmail *(1929). In* Torn Curtain *(1966) he shows up with a kid again, and, this time, the child wets on him. (Photofest)*

Saboteur (1942): in front of Cut Rate Drugs as the saboteur's car stops

Shadow of a Doubt (1943): in a card game on a train to Santa Rosa, California, with a full house in his potentially winning hand

Lifeboat (1944): in a newspaper ad as the "before" and "after" for the Reduco Obesity Slayer corset

Spellbound (1945): coming out of an elevator, carrying a violin case and smoking a cigarette

Notorious (1946): sips champagne at a party at Claude Rains' mansion

The Paradine Case (1948): walks through a door at England's Cumberland Station carrying a cello

Rope (1948): crossing the street after the opening credits, and in his trademark silhouette on a neon sign, about fifty-five minutes into the movie

Under Capricorn (1949): in the town square during a parade, wearing a blue coat and brown hat, then again, as one of three men on the stairs of Government House

Stage Fright (1950): walks by and looks back at Jane Wyman in her disguise as Marlene Dietrich's maid

Strangers on a Train (1951): boarding a train carrying a double bass as Farley Granger gets off in his hometown

89

ALFRED AND THE CHIPMUNK *When Alfred Hitchcock made one of his trademark cameos in* Rear Window *(1954), in the foreground is a musician who would find fame of his own: Ross Bagdasarian, creator of* Alvin and the Chipmunks *(1983). (Photofest)*

I Confess (1953): in silhouette in the distance, at the top of the stairs after the opening credits

Dial M for Murder (1954): a subtle appearance, in a photo held by Ray Milland

Rear Window (1954): seen winding a clock in the screenwriter's apartment (Note: the screenwriter is played by Ross Bagdasarian of "Alvin and the Chipmunks" fame!)

The Trouble with Harry (1955): walks past the parked limousine of a man who is looking at paintings in John Forsythe's outdoor exhibition

The Man Who Knew Too Much (1956): in the Moroccan marketplace, watching acrobats

The Wrong Man (1957): narrating the prologue; the only time he actually speaks during his films

Vertigo (1958): walks down the street past a subway entrance wearing a gray suit

North by Northwest (1959): misses a bus as it slams the door in his face during the opening credit sequence

Psycho (1960): seen through a window standing outside a realty office wearing a cowboy hat

The Birds (1963): passes by Tippi Hedren while walking two dogs (his own Sealyham terriers, Geoffrey and Stanley)

90

Marnie (1964): in a hotel corridor, just after Tippi Hedren passes by early in the movie

Torn Curtain (1966): sitting in a hotel lobby holding a baby, who wets on him

Topaz (1969): being pushed in a wheelchair through an airport, after which he gets up, shakes hands with a man, then walks away

Frenzy (1972): in the center of the crowd wearing a bowler hat, and is seen to be the only character not applauding the speaker

Family Plot (1976): in silhouette, obtaining copies of death certificates at the registrar's office

Two Hitchcock short films believed lost have recently resurfaced. *Aventure Malagra* and *Bon Voyage*, both filmed in 1944, apparently do not contain cameo appearances by the master of suspense.

NAME GAMES

*O*ne of the easiest places to create a cinematic inside joke is within a character or place name. After all, most of the time the sites and characters are fictional, so it's a perfect opportunity to name towns, buildings, or characters after friends, family, and occasionally, rivals.

As an example, director Joe Dante named almost everyone in his *The Howling* (1981), a film wherein most of the characters are werewolves, after famous directors who had made werewolf movies. Perhaps the most notable example is therapist Dr. George Waggner, played by Patrick Macnee. The real George Waggner directed the capstone of all werewolf features: *Wolf Man* (1941), starring Claude Rains. Others are Charles Barton, *Abbott and Costello Meet the Killer Boris Karloff* (1949); Terence Fisher, *Curse of the Werewolf* (1961); Freddie

Francis, *Legend of the Werewolf* (1975); Erle C. Kenton, *House of Frankenstein* (1944); Lew Landers, *Return of the Vampire* (1943); Jacinto Molina, *El Retorno de Hombre-Lobo* (1944); Roy William Neill, *Frankenstein Meets the Wolf Man* (1943); Sam Newfield, *The Mad Monster* (1942); and Jerry Warren, *Face of the Screaming Werewolf* (1959). In *The Howling*, co-writer John Sayles, later to become a noted film director in his own right, makes a hilarious cameo as a morgue attendant. In addition, Forrest J. Ackerman (editor of *Famous Monsters from Filmland* magazine) and penurious producer Roger Corman also turn up in the film.

More on the name game...

Twisting in the Wind

Jan de Bont, who helmed *Twister* (1996) and is an unabashed fan of fellow director Stanley Kubrick, named one of his characters in this storm thriller Stanley and another one Kubrick. Continuing the tribute, when a twister rips through a drive-in theatre, Kubrick's classic fright-film *The Shining* (1980) is playing on the big screen.

Quentin's Hawkish Airman

Recalling an airman named "Wynocki," who transports the watch to safety, Captain Koons (Christopher Walken) visits young Butch (Chandler Lindauer) in Quentin Tarantino's *Pulp Fiction* (1994) to give him his father's watch. The name "Wynocki" is John Garfield's character in director Howard Hawks' *Air Force* (1943). Hawks is one of Tarantino's favorite directors.

A Name He Couldn't Refuse

In *The Godfather Part II* (1974) Troy Donahue plays a character named Merle Johnson. It's a name to which he has no trouble answering. Merle Johnson is the name with which Donahue was born.

Adam and Heather

If the names of police officers Milner & McCord sound familiar in *Heathers* (1989), perhaps it's because they're named for Martin Milner and Kent McCord, stars of the first *Adam 12* (1968–75) TV police drama series.

George Is Back

If you're one of the twelve (or so) people who saw *Hudson Hawk* (1991), you might have noticed that James Coburn's character was named George Kaplan, the same as the fake government agent in *North by Northwest* (1959).

The Distaff Reporter

The Brothers Coen (Joel and Ethan) honored Army Archerd, perhaps today's best-known Hollywood columnist, when they named their own intrepid reporter Amy Archer (Jennifer Jason Leigh) in *The Hudsucker Proxy* (1994).

Born in a Bar

If you think you've heard the names of some of the characters in *Repo Man* (1984) recently, we know where you've been hanging out—Bud (Harry Dean Stanton), Miller (Tracy Walter), Lite (Sy Richardson)—they're beers, of course. Emilio Estevez, playing Otto, is asked his name by Oly (Tom Finnegan). When he says, "Otto," Oly says, "Otto Parts?" Later in the film we see Otto near a sign that reads "Auto Parts."

So Who Was Big Bird's Namesake?

Perhaps the two most famous television characters of all time are *Sesame Street*'s Ernie and Bert. Guess where the names came from? *It's a Wonderful Life* (1946). They were named for characters played by Frank Faylen (Ernie) and Ward Bond (Bert).

The Little Shop Vac Gets a Name

Perhaps the most famous name in sci-fi movies is rumored to have come about as a result of a conversation between George Lucas and a film editor. When they were editing *American Graffiti* (1973) an editor asked Lucas for "Reel 2, Dialog 2." The tape was labeled R2D2, and the name went into Lucas' script for *Star Wars* (1977), and, thence, on to film immortality.

One Thing Leads to Another

The nuclear submarine in *Crimson Tide* (1995) is the *Alabama*, whose state university football team is known as the Crimson Tide. We assume that's why the Captain's dog is named "Bear," as Alabama's football team was coached by the legendary Bear Bryant.

The Editor Takes a Chance

John Carpenter tips his hat to John Wayne in *Assault on Precinct 13* (1976). In the film's credits you'll see the

REMEMBERING 'BAMA *Director Tony Scott slipped several references to the University of Alabama's football team and its legendary coach, "Bear" Bryant, into his* Crimson Tide *(1995). (The Blackburn Archive)*

97

editor listed as "John T. Chance." That was Wayne's character name in *Rio Bravo* (1959), on which *Assault* is based; the editor is actually Carpenter himself.

We Found Him Hiding Again

Carpenter hid behind the name Edmund Dantes as one of the screenwriters of *Beethoven* (1992). Dantes was the character whose story is told in *The Count of Monte Cristo* (1908, 1913, 1934, 1954, 1961, and a TV movie in 1975).

And Again . . .

The writer in *Prince of Darkness* (1987) is listed as Martin Quatermass. It's actually John Carpenter, this time paying homage to the classic 1950s sci-fi horror character of British television.

Good Ole Earl

If you're a David Letterman fan, you'll probably recognize an inside joke as the reason that Letterman's character, the "Old Salt in the Fishing Village" is identified as Earl Hofert in the credits of *Cabin Boy* (1994). He called himself "Hofert" in some of his TV skits in the old NBC version (1982–93) of his late night talk show. In real life, we're told that Earl Hofert is his uncle on his mother's side. Letterman also takes the Hofert credit for his voice-over in the animated feature *Beavis and Butthead Do America* (1996).

And You Thought It Was That Nice Italian Boy from Brooklyn

The credits of *The Adventures of Baron Munchausen* (1989) list the character playing The Man on the Moon as Ray DiTutto. It's actually Robin Williams and the name refers to "Rei Di Tutto," translated "King of Everything," which is the way Williams' character introduces himself to the Baron.

Not a Pretty Sight

Christopher Walken's character in *Batman Returns* (1992) is named Max Schreck, for the actor who played the eeriest, ugliest vampire ever filmed, the subject of F. W. Murnau's *Nosferatu, eine Symphonie des Grauens* (1922).

The Evil Ssoj Dnulkca

Joss Acklund portrays the villain De Nomolos in *Bill and Ted's Bogus Journey* (1991). Check out the name. It's Ed Solomon, writer/producer of the film, spelled backwards. Incidentally, the teen comedy was originally titled *Bill and Ted Go to Hell*, but theatre owners were reluctant to put it up on their marquees, so the title was changed.

Colonel Backwards, Part Deux

Richard Crenna is Col. Denton Walters in *Hot Shots! Part Deux* (1993). In both the radio series (1948–57) and the TV version (1952–56) of *Our Miss Brooks* he played Walter Denton.

Bringing Up Jerry (Again)

In *Bringing Up Baby* (1938), Susan (Katharine Hepburn), pretending she and David (Cary Grant) are gangsters, tells the cops that David's underworld nickname is "Jerry the Nipper," the same nickname Grant had in *The Awful Truth* (1937).

Snipes Hunt

Wesley Snipes' character in *Drop Zone* (1994) is named Pete Nessip. Unscramble Nessip and you get Snipes.

So Who Gives the Orders?

David Carradine's onscreen alter ego in *Field of Fire* (1992) is named General Corman. Roger Corman was field general for the picture as one of the producers.

A Fish Called Archie

John Clease's screen personna in *A Fish Called Wanda* (1988) owes his name to Cary Grant. His character is called Archie Leach, Grant's real name. Kevin Kline, suggesting possible snitchers to George (Tom Georgeson), lists among them Kevin Delaney, which happens to be his own first and middle names.

Producer Promo

Billy says he bought a comic book at "Dr. Fantasy's" in *Gremlins* (1984). Dr. Fantasy is executive producer Frank Marshall's nickname. You can see the name also in *Poltergeist* (1982), produced by Marshall as well, when the outdoor marquee at the Holiday Inn is seen as "Welcome, Dr. Fantasy and Friends."

100

Then There Was That Rat Named Willard...

You never know where a writer will find inspiration for a character name. For example, Willard Huyck, one of the screenwriters on *Indiana Jones and the Temple of Doom* (1984) must have looked into his back yard. The character Short Round was named for his dog which, in turn, was named after the orphan (played by William Chun) in Samuel Fuller's *The Steel Helmet* (1951).

A Good Housekeeper Is Hard to Find

Assuming there's much behind-the-scenes housekeeping on a movie set, when the family in *Mrs. Doubtfire* (1993) is looking for Robin Williams' replacement, the last name they cross off the list is "Paula Dupré." She's the comedy's associate producer.

The Director's Revenge

If you wait long enough, you get your revenge. Word is that Wes Craven named his memorable *A Nightmare on Elm Street* (1984) creature Freddy Krueger after a kid who bullied him in school. Notice also that just before Glen (Johnny Depp) is pulled into bed, the TV station gives its call letters as KRGR.

The Really Big Lebowski
(aka Revenge of the Nerds Part Deux)

We don't know their motives for doing so, but the title character ("The Dude") of *The Big Lebowski* (1998) is

THE REAL REAL LEBOWSKI *Offbeat directors Joel and Ethan Coen may have named the title character, played by Jeff Bridges in* The Big Lebowski *(1998) for schoolmate Jeff Lebowksi, now assistant attorney general for the state of Minnesota. (The Blackburn Archive)*

101

named Jeffrey Lebowski, the same name as the thirty-seven-year-old assistant attorney general of Minnesota, home state of the quirky producer/writer/ director team of brothers Joel and Ethan Coen. Minnesota's Lebowski, who admits to being a party animal in his salad days, says with a laugh, "I guess they knew of my reputation." Their paths crossed in high school, where the Coens were in the same class as Lebowksi's older brother and sister.

Honoring Mary

One of the joys of living in Hollywood is you often get to meet genuine film legends. I once had the opportunity of meeting Mary Philbin, the original Christine of *The Phantom of the Opera* (1925). Brian de Palma remembered her in his *Phantom of the Paradise* (1974), a take-off on the original, by naming the studio owner, Philbin.

Initially Speaking

Steve Martin's *Roxanne* (1987) shares its basic plot with that of *Cyrano de Bergerac* (1950, etc.). Martin, playing C. D. Bales, also shares Cyrano's initials.

Digital Name Game

Moviedom's most famous computer very nearly shares a name with the digital world's most famous company. Take the name of "Hal" from *2001: A Space Odyssey* (1968) and move each letter up one character. What do you get? IBM.

Two Talons Down

During production of *Willow* (1988), the two-headed monster was named "The Siskbert" after a couple of well-known Chicago film reviewers (some sources also call it the "Ebersisk"). In the same fantasy adventure, the evil general Kael (Pat Roach) got his name from the ever-so-tough reviewer Pauline Kael.

It's a Wonderful Name

The character names for George (Matt Adler), Violet (Kelly Preston), and Mr. Gower (Ralph Bellamy) in John Landis' *Titan Man* segment of *Amazon Women on the Moon* (1987) all come from the beloved classic *It's a Wonderful Life* (1946).

103

Remembrances of Things Past

Harrison Ford's *Apocalypse Now* (1979) character honors George Lucas, who directed him in both *American Graffiti* (1973) and *Star Wars* (1977). His uniform bears the name tag "Col. G. Lucas." In the same production, G. D. Spradlin is General R. Corman, after famed cheapskate producer Roger Corman.

A Rocky Trip through Time

Jay Ward's characters from his *Rocky and His Friends* (1959–61) and *The Bullwinkle Show* (1961–73, 1981–82) have inspired many a writer and director, among them the creators of *Back to the Future* (1985). Farmer Peabody's son is named Sherman. Sherman (voiced by Walter Tetley) was the little boy who traveled through time in *Rocky and Bullwinkle*, and Peabody was the dog (voiced by Bill Scott) who owned the time machine.

A Brazilian Tribute

Before creating his offbeat film classics, director Terry Gilliam worked for Harvey Kurtzman's manic *Help!* magazine. There he met John Clease, who invited him to join the Monty Python troupe. In *Brazil* (1985), Gilliam named Ian Holm's character Mr. Kurtzmann, after his old employer.

Directing the Names

Stephen Norrington named some of his characters in *Death Machine* (1995) after other directors, including John Carpenter, Joe Dante, Sam Raimi, and Ridley Scott ("Scott Ridley" in the movie). The names Yutani and Weyland came from Scott's *Alien* (1979).

Son of Directing the Names

John Carpenter named the characters Romero (Frank Doubleday) and Cronenberg (John Strobel) for the directors of the same names in *Escape from New York* (1981), George Romero and David Cronenberg. The character Rehme (Tom Atkins) is for producer and former Motion Picture Academy President Robert Rehme.

Once Was Not Enough

Carpenter used the names of several members of the cast and crew of *Halloween* (1978) in *The Fog* (1980), including Nick Castle (Tom Atkins again), for the actor who played The Shape in the earlier movie and Tommy Wallace (played by George 'Buck' Flower) for *Halloween*'s production designer of the same name. Just to confuse things, the real Tommy Wallace appears as a ghost in *The Fog*, and actress Nancy Keyes shows up in both movies, as Sandy Fadel in *The Fog* and Annie Wallace in *Halloween*.

Fierce Actors

Much of the action in *Fierce Creatures* (1997) takes place in the Marwood Zoo, named, we presume, for John Marwood Cleese, who stars in the movie.

105

An Actor's Business

A store in *The Muppet Christmas Carol* (1992) is named Micklewhite's. Michael Caine, who plays Ebenezer Scrooge, was born Maurice Micklewhite.

Ben Did Better Later

Ben Affleck, whose career took a turn for the better when he and Matt Damon co-wrote and co-starred in *Good Will Hunting* (1997) played a character named Shannon Hamilton in *Mallrats* (1995). That would be the married name of the film's star, *Beverly Hills 90210* (1990–) bad girl Shannon Doherty, who was briefly married to George Hamilton's son Ashley. The names of the characters Brodie and Quint in *Mallrats* come from *Jaws* (1975), and Marvel Comics guru Stan Lee cameos in the film playing himself.

A Mouse in the House

Actor/screenwriter buddies Matt Damon and Ben Affleck named the characters played by Stellen Skarsgård and John Mighton (the professor and his assistant) in their Oscar-winning *Good Will Hunting* (1997) Gerry and Tom, after Hanna-Barbera's famous cat-and-mouse duo. Damon told *Entertainment Weekly* that the names were "an inside joke. We didn't think anyone would get it." Tom and Jerry were also the names of Noah Wylie's stoner friends in *The Myth of Fingerprints* (1997). Then again, there was that guy named Tom who played *Jerry McGuire* (1996)....

106

He Got Religion

John Turturro's character, Coach Billy Sunday, in *He Got Game* (1998) is a college basketball coach who uses prayer and religious fervor to recruit Jesus Shuttlesworth (Ray Allen) for his team. *Game's* writer/director Spike Lee obviously looked to the annals of American religious history for the character name. The Reverend Billy Sunday was perhaps America's best-known evangelist of the late nineteenth and early twentieth centuries, a fiery prohibitionist who was once a professional baseball player, leaving the Chicago White Stockings in 1891 to hit the sawdust trail.

THE ACTOR DID IT

*A*uthor Peter Hay tells of the speculation about the words that actors actually mouthed in the old silent movies in his wonderful *Movie Anecdotes* (Oxford University Press, 1990). He relates the story of the actor who was carrying a girl to her bed in a tender moment. As she is swooning with love, her lips read, "If you drop me, you bastard, I'll kill you."

It's a classic case of an actress slipping her own joke into a movie, and it happens more than you might realize. Sometimes it's with the complicity of the director; other times it is the work of a thespian slipping something past the system and right into the film.

Karl Malden creates inside jokes with his real name. Notice that in *On the Waterfront* (1954), Slim (Fred Gwynne) gives his name as "Malden Sekulovich." That's

PUBLICITY GAG
This isn't a scene from the film Mister Roberts *(1955). It's a gag publicity shot in which Henry Fonda's reading matter on board ship is the book upon which the film is based.*
(*JC Archives*)

a joke on costar Karl Malden's real name, Mladen Sekulovich. It's a joke he was said to slip into his *The Streets of San Francisco* (1972–77) TV series, often addressing a character passing on the street with "Hey, Sekulovich."

How to Deal with Trouble

When Tim Roth shoots a lady in *Reservoir Dogs* (1992) it's a rare case of onscreen revenge. The actress playing the part is his dialog coach, who was hard on him during production, so he insisted she play the role of the shooting victim.

Sleeping One's Way into the Movie

Tom Hanks, playing Sam Baldwin, says that Mary Kelly is the "eighth girl he slept with in college" in *Sleepless in Seattle* (1993). Mary Kelly was the film's script supervisor and had a cameo role as the nervous woman on the plane.

Did Sissy Do It?

Given that the role of Phoenix in *Phantom of the Paradise* (1974) was played by Jessica Harper, isn't it interesting that on her mirror is a magazine article headlined "I'm a Harper's Freak"? Isn't it also interesting that actress Sissy Spacek was the set decorator for the film? Hmmm... we find work where we can.

109

Elvis Lives ... in Ceramic

Peter Dobson played Elvis Presley in *Forrest Gump* (1994). Is that why there's an Elvis figurine in his bedroom in *The Frighteners* (1996), in which he plays Ray Linsky?

He'll Be Back ... Again ... and Again ... and Again ... and ...

Arnold Schwarzenegger seems to have adopted the "I'll be back" line from *The Terminator* (1984) as a personal trademark. It's as closely identified with Schwarzenegger as "Make my day" is to Clint Eastwood. In *Commando* (1985) Schwarzenegger says, "I'll be back, Bennet." He also uses the "I'll be back" sound bite in *Predator* (1987),

VOICE OF EVIL
Actor Brad Dourif slipped an inside joke into EXORCIST III: THE LEGION *(1990) with references to his providing the voice for the evil doll Chucky in the* Child's Play *movies. (The Blackburn Archive)*

The Running Man (1987), *Twins* (1988), *Terminator 2: Judgment Day* (1991), and in the spoof *Last Action Hero* (1993).

A Tribute to His Buddy

In *Four Men and a Prayer* (1938) David Niven says "I knew a man named Trubshawe..." The line refers to one of his lifelong friends whose name re-occurs in several of Niven's movies.

The Little (Road)House on the Beach

Given that Patrick Swayze starred in *Road House* (1989), we wonder if it's an inside joke or a coincidence that a scene in *Point Break* (1991) takes place at Patrick's

Roadhouse at the beach on Pacific Coast Highway in Santa Monica, where you can often see Arnold Schwarzenegger and other big stars breakfasting.

Hat Tricks

Burgess Meredith wore an old felt hat in Maxwell Anderson's *Winterset* (1935) on Broadway. After that it turned up again and again as a good luck charm in many of his films.

111

SCREENING WRITERS

*R*odney Dangerfield gets loads of respect compared to the average screenwriter. On a movie set, the writer usually watches quietly from the sidelines, if he or she is allowed on the set at all. Some directors won't let the scribe get anywhere near the script or the set once shooting begins. Writers are often so powerless that one of the oldest jokes in Hollywood is about the ingenue who was so stupid that she slept with the screenwriter.

Joseph L. Mankiewicz once called the screenwriter "the highest paid secretary in the world." Expressing another point of view, William Goldman said, "The only one who gets screwed around with is the writer, because everyone knows the alphabet." So it's a wonder when the writer gets a chance to make a sneak cameo in a film. Nonetheless, it happens, especially if he or she has gained fame in some medium other than screenwriting.

**Feeding Our Curiosity about the Future . . .
and the Pigeons**

One of the more distinguished writers to make a cameo appearance in a film based on his work is sci-fi award-winner Arthur C. Clarke, author of *The Sentinel* (a short story that appeared in his 1953 collection *Expedition to Earth*), on which *2001: A Space Odyssey* (1968) was based. In its movie sequel, *2010* (1984), Clarke is the kindly man sitting on a Washington park bench feeding the pigeons.

Playing His Hand

114

Look for playwright David Mamet, playing Herb, among the poker players at Alexandra's (Debra Winger) table in *Black Widow* (1987). Another prominent playwright, Harold Pinter, is a bookstore customer in *Turtle Diary* (1985), made from his quirky screenplay.

An Arresting Appearance

James Dickey worked himself into the script he wrote for *Deliverance* (1972), which he created from his novel (1970). Dickey is the gum-chewing Sheriff Bullard.

A Head-Spinning Project

William Peter Blatty, author of the 1971 novel on which *The Exorcist* (1973) is based, appears in the film adaptation as the producer of the film in which Chris (Ellen Burstyn) appears. In the book, the film she's producing is a musical version of *Mr. Smith Goes to Washington*

SHERIFF DICKEY *Author James Dickey wrote himself into*
Deliverance *(1972). He's the sheriff, seen here with Jon Voight.*
(Photofest)

(1939). Now that's a prospect that can send your head spinning!

Party Girl

The actress who plays Abby, both a big-haired recluse and a party girl, in *Slaves of New York* (1989), adapted from her book (published in 1986), is novelist Tama Janowitz herself. In a different vein, in Disney's *The Rocketeer* (1991), Dave Stevens, creator of the comic book on which the film is based, can be seen as the Nazi commander in the black-and-white test flight movie.

Party Girl: The Adventure Continues

In *The Joy Luck Club* (1993), Amy Tan, author of the novel (1989) on which the film was based, can be seen among the guests during the first party scene.

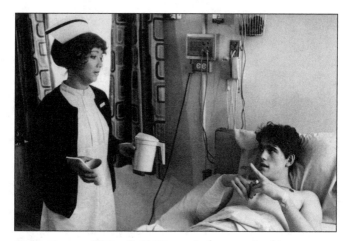

Nurse Hinton *Writer S. E. Hinton is the nurse in this scene with Matt Dillon in* The Outsiders *(1982), adapted from her novel. The author has appeared in three movies made from her novels. (Photofest)*

Prostituting Her Talent

Famed writer S. E. Hinton shows up as a hooker in *Rumble Fish* (1983). In Francis Ford Coppola's *The Outsiders* (1983), she's a nurse. In *Tex* (1982), she plays Mrs. Barnes. All of the films were made from her novels.

Refereeing the Project

Novelist John Irving plays a wrestling match referee in the filmed version (1982) of his *The World According to Garp* (1978).

Hammering Out a Role for Himself

Tough-guy novelist Mickey Spillane had a bit more than cameo roles in *The Girl Hunters* (1963), in which he played his fictional character Mike Hammer, and in *Ring of Fear* (1954) in which he played himself.

Winner of the Contest

One of the more odd writer cameos takes place in *Annie Hall* (1977). Truman Capote is seen walking through Central Park. Woody Allen's character describes him as "the winner of the Truman Capote look-alike contest." In the same Oscar-winning comedy are future stars Jeff Goldblum (in the party set in Los Angeles), Shelley Hack (on the street), Beverly D'Angelo (seen on a TV monitor), Sigourney Weaver (as Woody's date in a long shot near the end) and Christopher Walken (Annie's brother), all making cameo appearances.

117

A Veteran Writer

In *Born on the Fourth of July* (1989), Ron Kovic, on whose flinty biography (written in 1976) the movie is based, shows up as a World War II veteran in the parade near the beginning. In another interesting cameo, famed anti-war activist Abbie Hoffman appears as one of the war/draft protestors.

The Writer As Barfly

Novelist Charles Bukowski, whose battles with the bottle were filmed as *Barfly* (1987), can be seen in a quintessential setting in the movie. When Henry (Mickey Rourke) and Wanda (Faye Dunaway) meet for the first time at a sleazy lounge, Bukowski is right where he belongs, at the bar having a drink.

BEFORE THE PARADE PASSES BY *Tom Cruise plays writer Ron Kovic in this scene from* Born on the Fourth of July *(1989). In the same scene Kovic appears as one of the Vietnam War protestors. (The Blackburn Archive)*

Creepy Cameos

Perhaps the most ubiquitous of the authors who make onscreen cameo appearances is frightmeister Stephen King, who makes Hitchcockian walk-ons in most of the films made from his novels and short stories. In *Creepshow* (1982) he's the ill-fated rube Jordy Verrill, and his real-life son Joe is the boy at the beginning who collects *Creepshow* and voodoo dolls. In *Creepshow 2* (1987) King is the truck driver in the "Hitcher" segment. Watch *Maximum Overdrive* (1986), also King's directing debut, and you'll see him as the man sworn at by the bank ATM. In *Pet Sematary* (1989) he takes on a more righteous role as a minister.

She Wants to Be a Cameo

Writer/performer Betty Comden (of the writing team of Comden and Green) makes an appearance that's brief but pivotal in *Garbo Talks* (1984). Near the end of the film, she is seen as Garbo, the elusive screen legend.

Huzzah for the Writer

The 1885 newspaper editor in *Back to the Future Part III* (1990) is M. R. Gale, a tribute to screenwriter Robert Gale, who wrote the entire trilogy.

Finally...a Little Respect

Screenwriters do occasionally get a chance to appear on screen. In *Tootsie* (1982), Murray Schisgal, who co-wrote

CREEPY STEPHEN *Stephen King cameos as the creepy Jordy Verill in* Creepshow *(1982), made from his screenplay. (Photofest)*

the script with Larry Gelbart, appears among the party guests. William Wisher, co-writer of *Terminator 2: Judgment Day* (1991) appears in his film as a galleria photographer.

We Spoke Too Soon

For the ultimate statement of how Hollywood feels about its writers, take a look at *Jurassic Park* (1993). The first victim eaten by the T-Rex is David Koepp, who co-wrote the screenplay with Michael Crichton.

An Arresting Scribe

When a thief gets arrested in a bodega, the co-screen-writer of *Ransom* (1996) shows up to help out with the scene; that's Richard Price as Gary Sinise's fellow detective. Price makes it a habit to slip into a small role in most of the films he writes. He's a city clerk in *Kiss of Death* (1995), again a detective in *Mad Dog and Glory* (1993), a doctor in *Night and the City* (1992), an artist at an art opening in the "Life Lesson" segment of *New York Stories* (1989), the guy who calls his dad in *The Color of Money* (1986), and the bowling bankroller in *The Wanderers* (1979).

DRAWN INTO THE PICTURE

*A*nimators, being by nature fun-loving types, don't hesitate when they have the chance to draw a few jokes into their pictures. It's been going on since the early days of animation when artists made fun of their bosses and colleagues, often in character names or caricatures. Even the animated mega-productions made possible by the recent rebirth of the nearly lost art form have their share of in-jokes.

Among the cartoons into which Disney animators drew themselves is *Ferdinand the Bull* (1938) when, in the Parade of Toreadors, we see several of the famed "nine old men," including Ward Kimball, Fred Moore, Hamilton Luske, Vladimir (Bill) Tytla, and Art Babbit (who designed the characters). The Matador is a caricature of Walt Disney himself.

In *Fantasia* (1940) they named the sorcerer "Yen Sid." Spell that backwards and see what you get.

Look closely at *One Hundred and One Dalmatians* (1961), and you'll see several characters from *The Lady and the Tramp* (1955) in a shop window during a twilight sequence.

Disney's modern-day artists follow in the inky footsteps of their predecessors. The 1992 theatrical release *Aladdin* has scenes that are virtually family portraits of the animators and their friends. When Aladdin sidles into the crowd to get a better view of Prince Achmed, his rival for Jasmine's hand, the characters on either side of him are likenesses of producer/directors Ron Clements and John Musker. According to some Disney sources, the original plan was to have the two characters as Gene Siskel and Roger Ebert, who would give two thumbs down to the new suitor. However, the studio decided to avoid any possible rights clearance problems, (a bit odd, because they distribute the *Siskel & Ebert* TV series!) so the directors got a bit of onscreen immortality.

Among the forty thieves in the "Friends Like Me" song sequence is effects animator Dorse Lanpher. Likenesses of legendary animator Glenn Keane, along with colleagues Eric Goldberg and T. Daniel Hofstedt (with his son Daniel) show up in a crowd scene.

In another inside joke with all sorts of portent, animators union president Tom Sito is drawn into the action as Crazy Hakim, the used fertilizer dealer.

Disney's merchandisers got their due, too. The stack of blocks that Jasmine's father plays with sits on a toy of the Beast from *Beauty and the Beast* (1991). Toys representing Sebastian from *The Little Mermaid* (1989) and Pinocchio also make cameo appearances.

Toying with the Story

Even animators who rely on computers aren't above slipping little in-jokes into their work. *Toy Story* (1995), for example, is replete with them. Camera manager Julie MacDonald pestered the art director, Ralph Eggleston, to work her name into the movie, and he did just that. On Sid's backpack look for "Julie McBarfle has cooties."

The sheepdog-in-residence at California's Bay Area Pixar Studios, where *Toy Story* was animated, is named Molly. She gets her recognition in the license plate on the moving truck: MLY1K9. The moving company is named Eggman Movers for the aforementioned Eggleston. Another license plate in the film is "HTT1195," incorporating the name of the production company–High Tech Toons–and the film's release date.

Director John Lasseter also slipped a few subtle references to his previous work in *Toy Story*. When Woody calls a meeting to announce Andy's birthday, a book in the background is entitled *Tin Toy* (1988), one of Lasseter's award-winning short films. Later in the scene another book bears the title *Knickknack* (1989), another of his animated shorts. The cute little desk lamp from

Luxo, Jr. (1986) also makes a cameo appearance in *Toy Story*.

Belle Reincarnated

The lovely Belle from *Beauty and the Beast* (1991) makes a cameo appearance in *The Hunchback of Notre Dame* (1996). She can be seen in the crowd reading a book while Quasimodo sings "Out There." Tone Thyne, assistant production manager on *Hunchback*, told *Entertainment Weekly*, "one of our storyboard artists included her in there as a joke, because both pictures take place in France." Even though the stories are set centuries apart, he says, "she told us it was Belle's great-great-grandmother."

124

Getting a Clearer Picture

The animators slipped a roof-top satellite dish into the same scene from *Hunchback*. Also, Pumba from *The Lion King* (1994) is carried by two men on a pole, and a merchant shakes out the flying carpet from *Aladdin* (1992).

Do You Know the Way To . . .

Disney's animators had their fun with *Beauty and the Beast* (1991). When old Maurice (voiced by Rex Everhart) is lost on horseback, he sees a directional sign pointing to Newhall, Valencia, and Anaheim. The California Institute of the Arts (aka "CalArts"), virtually a branch of the Disney studios and alma mater of many of its animators, is located near Newhall and Valencia, California. As for Anaheim, well . . .

A Beastly End

Another *Beauty and the Beast* (1991) joke may or may not be there, depending on how you view the animated feature. It's alleged that the Beast has a heart-shaped tattoo on his tuchis in one frame of the film. However, it's apparently only in the "work in progress" laserdisc version; his nether parts are obscured by his cape in the final release.

The Boss Is Skeptical

Peter Schneider, Disney's president of feature animation, gets into the picture in *Oliver & Company* (1988). He's drawn in as the skeptical pawnbroker.

Who Among Us Could Disagree?

Anaheim's best-known attraction is worked into *The Lion King* (1994). When Scar (voiced by Jeremy Irons) asks a prisoner to sing for him, he breaks into "It's a Small World," theme song of the park's kiddie attraction. As have millions of parents, Scar says, "No, no. Anything but that!"

Disney's best-known trademark gets its due in the same movie. One of the bugs that Timon pulls out of a knothole during "Hakuna Matata" is wearing mouse ears.

Those Pesky Rumors

We can't leave this topic without discussing some of the animation jokes that weren't and some that might have been.

Perhaps the most talked about is the apparent appearance of the word "SEX" in the sky as Pumba, Simba, and Timon relax on their backs in *The Lion King* (1994). If you look really, really hard you just might see the three letters in the dust cloud that drifts away after the trio flops down. It's also reported that the letters are "S-F-X" for "special effects."

This is but one of those rumors that twisted the drawers of the anti-Disney fanatics and worked them up into a self-righteous snit. Think of it what you will, but it's really hard to believe that a major corporation like Disney, whose fortunes are built on entertainment for young children, would let its animators get away with something like that, either by default or by design.

Similarly conceived was the story that an artist deliberately drew a penis as one of the towers of the castle on the promotional artwork for *The Little Mermaid* (1989). This one's a bit harder to argue, as one of the towers bears a remarkable resemblance to an erect Johnson. However, we spoke to an artist who worked in the studio where the artwork was created, and he swears it was purely a coincidence. Contrary to rumor, the artist wasn't unhappy with Disney, nor was his job in jeopardy either before or after the incident.

Nonetheless, it led some video stores to pull the cassette from their shelves temporarily, and the artwork was revised for the laserdisc version.

Walt Disney
was a tough
employer, but
he couldn't stop
his animators
from slipping
inside jokes
into the studio's
cartoons.
(Photofest)

127

Ward Kimball, seen here, with his boss Walt Disney, was one of the
studio's legendary "nine old men" depicted in Ferdinand the Bull
(1938). (Photofest)

Doing It Like a Wabbit

If you really have a yearning to see an animator's concept of the male organ (and don't want to rent Ralph Bakshi's *Fritz the Cat* (1972), take a look at the cartoon *The Wabbit Who Came to Dinner* (1948). You'll have to go frame by frame to find it, but when Bugs Bunny steps out of the shower and wraps a towel around himself (an oddity in itself, because the wascally wabbit usually doesn't wear clothes) for but a moment the towel slips and you see something between his legs that indicates the sport for which bunny rabbits have long been famous.

Jessica's Dirty Little Secrets

While we're waxing anatomical, much has been written about some animated lewdness in *Who Framed Roger Rabbit* (1988). Several jokes of a less-than-savory nature are supposedly hidden within the movie and can only be seen on a laserdisc or a high-quality VCR.

Again, snits and fits were tossed when word got out about Jessica Rabbit's sordid little secrets, but if they existed they seem to have been corrected before the film went to video. Among the alleged shots are one where Jessica's underwear seems to disappear when she's thrown from a taxi. An intrepid fan of the movie says that it's a shadowy, ambiguous image at best and appears to be more of a paint error than an intentional joke.

Another is a shot of men's room graffiti that says "For a Good Time Call Allyson Wonderland" and "The Best Is

Yet to Be." Word has it that (Disney chairman) Michael Eisner's home telephone number was written beneath it. Again, if it was ever there, our researchers say it's been erased from the video/laser release.

However, one shot remains onscreen which surely seems to be a deliberate in-joke. At the beginning of the film, Baby Herman stomps off the set and goes under a woman's dress. If you check it out frame-by-frame, you'll see him extend his middle finger just before going under the skirt, and coming out with a spot of drool on his upper lip. Score one for the animators.

PROPPING IT UP

One of the more subtle ways filmmakers slip inside jokes into their films is in props and set decorations. It can be a photo on a desk, a film poster, a painting on a wall, even a tombstone. Yep. A tombstone. Take a look at the graveyard in *Arsenic and Old Lace* (1944). Cary Grant sits on a tombstone outside his daft aunts' home. The name on another is "Archie Leach," Grant's real name. In an earlier move, *His Girl Friday* (1940), Grant tells of the horrible fate suffered by a man who once crossed him...a man named "Archie Leach."

It can be a prop newspaper. A news story in a paper seen in Orson Welles' mutilated masterpiece, *The Magnificent Ambersons* (1942) shows the byline "Jed Leland." Leland was a character in Welles' *Citizen Kane* (1941).

It can even be a character mask. We're told that the flashing eyes of the Borg in *Star Trek: First Contact* (1996) list the names of people associated with the production in Morse code. If you can read Morse code, check it out for yourself. Our grasp of the dots and dashes is pretty limited. By the way, if you're ever in Hollywood at night or see a live picture of our city, check out the flashing warning light atop the famous Capital Records Tower on Vine Street. It spells out "Hollywood" in Morse code, sort of a civic inside joke.

Scent of a Bullet

The T-800 robot (Arnold Schwarzenegger) in *Terminator 2: Judgment Day* (1991) carries a gun in a box of roses. We're talking really subtle here, because parts of the sound track features Guns n' Roses.

She's Having a Beamer

Check out the license plate on the BMW in *She's Having a Baby* (1988). It's SHAB, an acronym of the film's title.

Lost and Found

The ark from *Raiders of the Lost Ark* (1981) and the famous sled *Rosebud* from *Citizen Kane* (1941) can be seen in the warehouse scene in *Honey, I Blew Up the Kid* (1992).

Searching for a Serial Joker

There wasn't much to laugh at in the Disney live-action comedy *Man of the House* (1995), starring Chevy Chase and Jonathan Taylor-Thomas, so at least the filmmakers peppered it with a few good inside jokes. When Taylor-Thomas, playing Ben Archer, thumbs through a list of serial killers, you'll see the name "Starling, Robin Anne Clarice." Jodie Foster played Clarice Starling in *The Silence of the Lambs* (1991), which, as an aside, was written by Thomas Harris, a kid who sat across the room from me in our high school English class deep in darkest Mississippi. Taylor-Thomas plays one of Tim Allen's sons in the *Home Improvement* (1991–) TV sitcom, so when he looks at a copy of *Life* magazine, the cover story is about dream houses. In addition, honoring his role as the voice of young Simba in *The Lion King* (1994), also a Disney movie, there's an ad for that animated feature on the back of the magazine.

133

Sneaking into Battle

A careful freeze-frame search of the view from Lando Calrissian's (Billy Dee Williams) cockpit during one of the battles in *Return of the Jedi* (1983) shows one of the spaceships that sustains a hit is actually a tennis shoe slipped into the shot by the special effects guys. It's hard to find, but we've seen it. It's there.

The Band of Avon

The bandstands in the acclaimed film of Shakespeare's *Richard III* (1995), updating the original play to World War II, bear the initials "WS," a homage, we suppose, to the original author William Shakespeare.

As Written by the Venus de Milo

One of the books on the can that traps Ash's possessed hand in *Evil Dead II* (1987) is Ernest Hemingway's 1929 novel *A Farewell to Arms*.

The Ex Files

A card index kept by the Death Secretary character in *Phantom of the Paradise* (1974) contains the names of Alice Cooper, David Geffen, Bette Midler, Peter Fonda, Dick Clark, and Kris Kristofferson.

From One Detective to Another

134

The book that Mrs. Houston (Lisa Kaye) is reading at her desk in the TV movie *The Return of Sherlock Holmes* (1987) was written by a well-known detective, none other than Jessica Fletcher, the fictional character played by Angela Lansbury in the *Murder, She Wrote* (1984–96) TV series.

Winnie the Ewok

Look carefully at one of the matte (background) paintings in TV's *The Ewok Adventure* (1984) and you just might find Winnie the Pooh sitting in a tree.

Films We Probably Won't Be Seeing (If We're Lucky)

Signs in a video store in *The Lost World: Jurassic Park* (1997) tout a trio of movies we don't expect to be seeing anytime soon: *King Lear*, starring Arnold Schwarzenegger; *Jack and the Behnstacks*, starring Robin Williams; and *Tsunami Surprise*, with Tom Hanks' head superimposed on a surfer's body.

Our Elected Unofficial

One of our friends is an actor named Don Snell. We accused him of bribing the prop man when he appeared in the Congressional hearing scene in *Contact* (1997). He sits behind a name plaque which reads "Senator Snell."

Name Plaques: The Sequel

A name plate on the guidance counselor's desk in *The Breakfast Club* (1985) reads "R. Hashimoto," the name of the film's production supervisor. Also in *The Breakfast Club*, an election poster for the prom queen names Michelle Manning, co-producer of the film.

One Man's Hero...

Stanley Kauffman reported in *The New Republic* that he caught an in-joke in *Jurassic Park* (1993). On the desk of the film's villain, a traitor, is a photo of J. Robert Oppenheimer. Oppenheimer, known as "the father of the atomic bomb," was accused of treachery during the red-baiting political era after World War II.

From One Alien to Another

Check out the plants in the garden in *E.T.: The Extra-Terrestrial* (1982) and you'll see a Triffid from the British sci-fi classic *The Day of the Triffids* (1963).

Read It and Weep

The sign on the bus just before the four main characters die in *Heart and Souls* (1993) is "4 Terminal."

Sound Advice

When Dr. Juliette Faxx reprograms the robot in *RoboCop 2* (1990), the numbers that scroll across the screen are 50 45 54 45 20 4B 55 52 41 4E 20 49 53 20 41 20 47 52 45 41 54 20 47 55 59. These are the computer hex codes for "Pete Kuran is a great guy." Kuran was the special effects photographer for the movie.

Life's Little Instruction List

We don't have the time or the patience to check it out, (in fact, we wonder about the person who did!), but we're told by an erstwhile contributor to the Internet Movie Database (IMDB) that among the instructions being programmed into the robot in *RoboCop 2* are:

DIRECTIVE 233: restrain hostile feelings

DIRECTIVE 234: promote positive attitude

DIRECTIVE 235: suppress aggressiveness

DIRECTIVE 236: promote pro-social values

DIRECTIVE 238: avoid destructive behavior

DIRECTIVE 239: be accessible

DIRECTIVE 240: participate in group activities

DIRECTIVE 241: avoid interpersonal conflicts

DIRECTIVE 242: avoid premature value judgments

DIRECTIVE 243: pool opinions before expressing yourself

DIRECTIVE 244: discourage feelings of negativity and hostility

DIRECTIVE 245: if you haven't got anything nice to say don't talk

DIRECTIVE 246: don't rush traffic lights

DIRECTIVE 247: don't run through puddles and splash pedestrians or other cars

DIRECTIVE 248: don't say that you are always prompt when you are not

DIRECTIVE 249: don't be oversensitive to the hostility and negativity of others

DIRECTIVE 250: don't walk across a ballroom floor swinging your arms.

DIRECTIVE 254: encourage awareness

DIRECTIVE 256: discourage harsh language

DIRECTIVE 258: commend sincere efforts

DIRECTIVE 261: talk things out

DIRECTIVE 262: avoid Orion meetings

DIRECTIVE 266: smile

DIRECTIVE 267: keep an open mind

DIRECTIVE 268: encourage participation

DIRECTIVE 273: avoid stereotyping

DIRECTIVE 278: seek nonviolent solutions

Directive 262 is perhaps the most telling. Orion is the studio which released the film, and studio interfer-

ence could blow the circuits on even the most sophisti-
cated robot.

Egg the Night Away

The crew of *The Rocky Horror Picture Show* (1975) had
an Easter egg hunt on the set, and they didn't find all the
eggs, but the camera did. One can be seen under Frank's
throne, one is in a light fixture in the main room, and one
can be seen as the group goes into an elevator to the lab.

Going Toward the Light

John Carpenter helmed *Big Trouble in Little China*
(1986). How do we know? Well, there's his credit, of
course. Then there's the light pattern that forms the Chinese symbol for "Carpenter" as it fades into another shot.

138

He Drove Them Crazy

When you see the sign for "Shady Acres Mental Hospital"
in *Ace Ventura: Pet Detective* (1994), you're seeing a dubi-
ous tribute to the movie's director, Tom Shadyac.

A Dubious Honor

One of the tombstones in *Tales from the Crypt Presents
Bordello of Blood* (1996) bears the name "Gaines."
William Gaines was publisher of the *Tales from the Crypt*
comic books.

An American Werewolf in Space

When George Lucas' costume people were suiting up
the bizarre creatures in the cantina scene in *Star Wars*

(1977), they ran out of masks... so one of the characters is wearing a standard joke-shop werewolf mask.

The Scariest Mask They Could Find

John Carpenter's *Halloween* (1978) was made on a shoe-string budget, so there was no money for elaborate masks and costumes. That's why they went to a costume store and bought a William Shatner mask, painted it white, and teased out the hair.

A Street Sign Named Kubelski

Jack Benny was one of the stars of the original *To Be or Not to Be* (1942), so when the film was remade in 1983 (this time starring Mel Brooks in the Benny role) a street sign reads "Kubelski Avenue." Jack Benny's real name was Benny Kubelski.

Now We Know Where It Is

The evil scientist of the title displays his penchant for purloined art in the first James Bond spy film, *Dr. No* (1962). A portrait of the Duke of Wellington, stolen in 1960 and never recovered, hangs in his headquarters.

Communicating One's Name

Near the end of *GoldenEye* (1995) a computer displays "Pevsner Communications GrnBH." Tom Pevsner was executive producer of the James Bond thriller.

The Writing on the Wall

When the ark is moved in *Raiders of the Lost Ark* (1981), if you're very sharp eyed and have a very good copy of the

Indiana Jones adventure, you might be able to see R2D2 and C3PO from *Star Wars* (1977) giving a trinket to an Egyptian mystic in the hieroglyphics on a column to the right. They're almost impossible to see on home video, so if you want to rent a theatre and check it out, go for it!

The Writing on the Wall: Part Deux

Check out the graffiti on the alley wall behind the dancing punks in *Repo Man* (1984) and you'll see "Circle Jerks," the name of the band who appears later in the movie.

Son of the Writing on the Wall

140

When Clint Eastwood is being chased by Scorpio in *Dirty Harry* (1972), he passes a wall in which his real-life son Kyle's name is painted.

MARQUEE MARKS

*T*ime was that, if a theatre marquee happened to appear in a Warner Bros. movie, it would read *Another Dawn*. There was no such movie; instead, it was a studio tradition that it appear. But back in 1937 director William Dieterle was unable to come up with a suitable title for a film he was making with Kay Francis and Errol Flynn. The studio decided to call it *Another Dawn* and the fictional title became a reality. Since then directors have had all sorts of fun with marquees.

Nowadays, when a theatre marquee happens to be in a shot, it's fair game for a director to use it to promote his past and future work as well as to salute that of his friends, and it's a surefire site for a plethora of in-jokes.

Check out the movie theatre marquee behind Clint Eastwood in Don Siegel's *Dirty Harry* (1972). It's adver-

A DIRTY JOKE *It may be Don Siegel's* Dirty Harry *(1972), but the theater behind Clint Eastwood is advertising a film Eastwood directed in 1971.* (Photofest)

tising *Play Misty for Me* (1971), directed by Eastwood and featuring Siegel in a cameo role as a bartender.

Here are other coming attractions via the marquee:

Cannibalizing the Moment

Take a look at the marquee on a Times Square grindhouse during *Ghostbusters II* (1989). It's promoting *Cannibal Girls*, a 1973 low-budget effort of *Ghostbusters II* director Ivan Reitman and SCTV friends Andrea Martin and Eugene Levy.

Double Feature Dèjá Vu

In both *Gremlins* (1984) and *Back to the Future* (1985) the main street is the same, and the town's movie theatre is showing a double feature: *A Boy's Life* with *Watch the Skies*.

Steven Spielberg was executive producer of both movies, and *A Boy's Life* was the working title for *E.T.: The Extra-Terrestrial* (1982). *Watch the Skies* was the working title for *Close Encounters of the Third Kind* (1977).

Forward to the Future

A subtle in-joke is slipped onto a marquee in *Back to the Future Part II* (1989), also executive-produced by Spielberg. The advertised film is *Jaws 19*, directed by Max Spielberg. Max is Steven Spielberg's real-life son, and his dad, of course, directed *Jaws* (1975).

LOOKING BACK *In Ivan Reitman's* Ghostbusters II *(1989) a theatre marquee in New York's Times Square advertises one of Reitman's early efforts,* Cannibal Girls *(1973). (Collection of the Author)*

Watch the Marquee *The movies on this marquee in* Gremlins *(1984) are the working titles for Steven Spielberg's* E. T.: The Extra-Terrestrial *(1982) and* Close Encounters of the Third Kind *(1977). (Video screen photo, collection of the author)*

Coming Attractions

Back in Times Square, dinosaurs dance around the famed intersection in *We're Back: A Dinosaur's Story* (1993). Once again, Spielberg was the executive producer. It was the same year that he released another dinosaur picture, so a theatre marquee in the background touts *Jurassic Park* (1993).

Coming Attractions: The Sequel

Roland Emmerich slips a quickie into *Independence Day* (1996). Not only does a bus crash through a billboard advertising *Stargate* (1994), his previous feature, but a marquee says "Coming Soon: *Independence Day*."

An Unimaginable Horror

As Sam (Hugh Grant) and Rebecca (Julianna Moore) rush home in Chris Columbus' *Nine Months* (1995) they pass a movie theatre advertising *Home Alone VII* (God help us!). *Home Alone* (1990) and *Home Alone 2: Lost in New York* (1992) were also directed by Columbus.

Pimping One's Self

Director Ken Russell does a bit of pimping for his previous work in *Whore* (1991). You can see theatres advertising his previous films *Crimes of Passion* (1984) and *The Lair of the White Worm* (1988).

Flying By

Richard Donner directed *Lethal Weapon* (1987) and *LW2* (1989). So, in *LW3* (1992) we can hardly be surprised when Murtagh (Danny Glover) and Riggs (Mel Gibson) pass a theatre and it's advertising *Radio Flyer* (1992), another Donner film!

The Donner Blitz

Richard Donner's first-of-the-series *Lethal Weapon* (1987) is not without a bit of cross-promotion as well. A marquee in the background of that movie reads "*The Lost Boys*: This Year's Hit." Donner executive-produced *Boys*, which was also released in 1987. Both were Warner

145

Bros. pictures, so score one for the studio marketing department.

Dèjá Now

When we see Mann's Chinese Theatre in Spike Lee's *Girl 6* (1996), it's advertising the current attraction: *Girl 6*. Hmmm.

These Buds Are for Me

It's not at a movie theatre, but the marquee at the sports arena where Butch (Bruce Willis) boxes in Quentin Tarentino's *Pulp Fiction* (1994) lists two fights: "Coolidge vs. Wilson" (both American presidents, of course), and "Vossler vs. Martinez." Rand Vossler and Jerry Martinez are long-standing friends of Tarentino, going back to the days when he worked in a video store. Tarentino also used the name "Vossler" for a character in *Crimson Tide* (1995); he was the script doctor for the submarine thriller, hired to punch up the dialog.

146

LISTENING
FOR THE JOKE

*S*ounds, heard either in the foreground or behind the scenes, offer a fertile field for a film's inside jokes. It can be a line of dialog, a public address system announcement, or the selection of a song with a particular meaning.

One of our favorites takes place in *The Big Easy* (1987), which is set, of course, in New Orleans. In the background, when Anne (Ellen Barkin) is on the phone, you can hear music from the fourth act of Giacomo Puccini's opera *Manon Lescaut* (1893), also set in New Orleans. We don't really know if it was a joke or just geographical ignorance on Puccini's part, but when the lovers in *Manon* leave the city, their next scene (where they succumb to the usual final operatic death) is in the desert. In Louisiana?

Listen for these:

147

Has Anyone Seen This Man?

In airport scenes in *Into the Night* (1985) and *Coming to America* (1988), both directed by John Landis, a "Mr. Frank Ozkerwitz" is being paged. That's the real name of fellow director (and the *real* Miss Piggy) Frank Oz.

Shine On

Because there's such a strong connection between werewolves and the full moon, John Landis made an audible homage to the legend in his film *Innocent Blood* (1992). All the songs in the movie have "moon" in their titles, including versions of "Blue Moon" by Bobby Vinton, Sam Cook, and The Marvels; "Bad Moon Rising" by Credence Clearwater Revival, and "Moondance" by Van Morrison.

Positive Identification

When Danny Glover, playing a bank robber, and Mel Gibson, playing the title character, appear to recognize each other in *Maverick* (1994), perhaps it's because they appeared together in *Lethal Weapon* (1987), *Lethal Weapon 2* (1989) and *Lethal Weapon 3* (1992). While they're together on screen, you can hear the *Lethal Weapon* theme song!

Sounds Familiar

Mel Gibson's character Tom comes up with the pseudonym "John Smith" in *Ransom* (1996). On the one hand, it's a fairly common name; on the other, it's the character for whom he provided the voice in Disney's animated *Pocahontas* (1995).

They Got 'Im

When the actor playing Richie is arrested in *Blown Away* (1994), a police radio can be heard in the background announcing the arrest of Dr. Richard Kimble (from the TV series *The Fugitive*, which ran from 1963–67).

And Again . . . and Again

In *The Day the Earth Stood Still* (1951) the words "Klaatu, Barada, Nikto" were used to direct the robot Gort. In *Army of Darkness* (1993) Ash, played by Bruce Campbell, uses those same words to claim *The Book of the Dead*. In *Toys* (1992), they're the words used by the General (Michael Gambon) to stop the sea creature's rampage. In *Return of the Jedi* (1983), three of the characters in Jabba the Hut's entourage are Klaatu, Barada, and Nikto.

149

The Doctors Are Stooges

In Garry Marshall's *Young Doctors in Love* (1982) you can hear a page for "Dr. Howard, Dr. Fine, Dr. Howard." It's the same page you can hear in several of The Three Stooges movies, beginning with *Men in Black* (1934). The Stooges were, of course, Moe Howard, Larry Fine, and Curly Howard.

AMERICA'S WORST DIRECTOR

With the possible exception of Edward D. Wood Jr. (*Plan 9 from Outer Space*, 1959; *Glen or Glenda*, 1953) no Hollywood director has been more reviled than Alan Smithee. *Premiere* magazine said "His name in the movie credits usually means disaster at the box office." Another prominent director said, "Smithee is a badge that says 'This picture is fucked up.'" Even his own union, the Director's Guild of America (DGA), says that discussing his work is "a sore point."

Yet the wide-ranging director (whose name appears in the credits of major motion pictures, B-movies, TV Movies-of-the-Week and even sitcom episodes) has, from time to time, drawn critical praise for his work. Reviewing his first film, *Death of a Gunfighter* (1969), the *New York Times* said, "The film has been sharply directed by Alan Smithee . . . [he] has an adroit facility for scanning faces and extracting sharp background detail." *Variety's* review of the same film said, "Smithee's direction keeps the action taut and he draws convincing portrayals from the supporting cast."

If you believe that Alan Smithee actually helmed any of the films that bear his name, you've become the victim of Hollywood's biggest and best-known inside joke.

Alan Smithee does *not* exist. His is the name that says the *real* director wants to disavow his own work, to take his name off the film and assign it to cinematic purgatory in the *nom de screen* of "Alan Smithee."

Smithee's reviled name (whose first name is sometimes spelled Allen, or Alan, or Allan) came to be when Don Siegel replaced Robert Totten as director of *Death of a Gunfighter* (1969), which starred Richard Widmark and Lena Horne. Both directors, miffed by Widmark's running roughshod over their work (the actor's contract gave him creative control), wanted their names taken off the project.

152

But a film has to be directed by somebody, so the Directors Guild of America (DGA) came up with the name "Alan Smith." John Rich, a member of the DGA Director's Council, said that someday there just might be a director with the name "Alan Smith," and suggested "Alan Smithee," thinking that it would be unusual enough not to be someone's real moniker. Oddly enough, someone somewhere actually took the time to analyze the name and put forth the theory that it arose as an anagram of "The Alias Men," but its true origins are in the more mundane workings of a committee meeting.

Since that time the fictitious Smithee has built up an impressive body of work. John Frankenheimer hid behind the name on *Riviera*, a 1987 TV pilot. Jud Taylor, a sought-after movie director, has been Smithee twice: for the theatrical film *Fade In* (1968) and the made-for-television film *City in Fear* (1980). Stuart Rosenberg used the Smithee sidestep when he was embarrassed by studio changes to the Mark Harmon vehicle, *Let's Get Harry* (1986). In another instance, David Lynch, unhappy with the addition of fifty minutes of excised footage to a televised version of his *Dune* (1984), opted to remove his name and let good ol' Alan Smithee take the credit, or the blame.

Joe Eszterhas' 1998 slap at Hollywood, *An Alan Smithee Film: Burn Hollywood Burn* provides the most ironic use of the name. It's the story of a director actually named Alan Smithee (Eric Idle) who wants to take his name off his film, but finds that if he does, it will still be directed by Alan Smithee. So he burns it, setting off a tale that rips into almost every aspect of Hollywood's peculiar culture. This movie fiasco was directed by the esteemed Arthur Hiller. Embarrassed by the finished product (even though he makes a cameo appearance near the end), Hiller took his name off *Burn*. Thus we have a film about a fictitious Alan Smithee, directed by a kinda sorta real-life Alan Smithee.

The DGA doesn't make it easy for a director to make the metamorphosis to Alan Smithee. The filmmaker

154

AMERICA'S WORST DIRECTOR   *Director Alan Smithee is responsible for some of the worst movies ever to sully the big screen. In this scene from* An Alan Smithee Film: Burn Hollywood Burn *(1998) the director, played by Eric Idle, does the right thing. He takes his film to the La Brea tar pits and burns it. (The Blackburn Archive)*

must go before a committee and supply evidence that his or her work has been brutalized. If the committee agrees but the production company protests, the matter has to go before yet another board comprised of representatives of the DGA and the Association of Motion Picture and Television Producers (AMPTP).

The wounded director then has a Hobson's choice: in accepting "Smithee" as a bandage for his grievances, he or she agrees not to speak to the press about the film for at least six months. However, when the embargo is lifted, the venom can flow. In 1988, Stuart Rosenberg told *Premiere* magazine about the *Let's Get Harry* (1986) debacle. "They totally mutilated the film. I've been in this business 37 years. I've never been treated with such total disrespect." Another director vented to the DGA's house magazine: "I'm on the canvas and I'm trying to get up. We started out with something good. Then other people came along and everything changed. It's a completely different movie. *My* film will never be seen."

Don Siegel noted with wry amusement that even though he had taken the Smithee pseudo-credit for *Death of a Gunfighter* (1969), the western nonetheless was well reviewed. "I told my young friends who wanted to be directors to change their name to Smithee and take credit for direction of the picture," he remarked. "I don't know if anyone did this. I still think under certain circumstances they might have cracked the 'magic barrier' and become directors."

We note with some amusement that one of the celluloid horrors attributed to Mr. Smithee is the TV movie *The O. J. Simpson Story* (1994), from which Jerrold Freedman took a directorial Bronco ride.

Smithee has also made forays into writing, acting, and production design. Ivan and Sam Raimi were identified as Alan Smithee Sr. and Jr. among the writers of *The Nutt House* (1995). Masato Harado took the moniker as both writer and director for the U.S. version of *Ganheddo* (1989), as did Gianni Bozzachi for *I Love N.Y.*

(1987). Smithee also has an actor credit in *Flynn* (1996) and *Blades* (1989).

While we're at it, we should point out that Smithee is not the only fake name that has made a significant impact on film history. When writer Robert Towne was dissatisfied with the way *Greystoke: The Legend of Tarzan of the Apes* (1984) turned out, he used the name of his sheepdog P. H. Vazak for the screenwriter credit. In a strange twist of fate, Vazak became the first (and, we assume, the only) sheepdog ever nominated for an Academy Award.

If you chance upon any of these films or TV episodes, you'll witness the work of the director of a cinematic sinking ship, one whose *oeuvre* was jokingly praised as intensely "celluloidal" by writer Nick Redman in the *DGA News*. View at your own risk!

An Alan Smithee Filmography

(Real Director, If Known, Listed in **Bold**)

An Alan Smithee Film: Burn Hollywood Burn (1998) **Arthur Hiller**

Firehouse (1997)

Le Zombi de Cap-Rouge (1997)

Sub Down (1997) **Gregg Champion**

Hellraiser: Bloodline (1996) **Kevin Yagher**

The O. J. Simpson Story (1994) (TV) **Jerrold Freedman**

Raging Angels (1995)

The Birds 2: Land's End (1994)
Rick Rosenthal

Gypsy Angels (1994)

While Justice Sleeps (1994) (TV)

Call of the Wild (1993) (TV) **Michael Uno**

Bay City Story (1992) (TV)

Fatal Charm (1992) (TV) **Fritz Kiersch**

Scent of a Woman (1992) [Airline Cut Only]
Martin Brest

Starfire (1992) **Richard Sarafian**

Thunderheart (1992) (TV) **Michael Apted**

The Owl (1991) (TV)

Bloodsucking Pharaohs in Pittsburgh (1990)
Dean Tschetter

Bodyguard (1990) (TV) [Pilot episode]

The Shrimp on the Barbie (aka *Boyfriend from Hell*) (1990) **Michael Gottlieb**

Solar Crisis (1990) **Richard C. Sarafian**

Backtrack (aka *Catchfire*) (1989)
Dennis Hopper

Ganheddo (1989) **Masato Harada**

The Horror Show (1989) [Smithee as writer only]

157

Death of a Gunfighter (*1969*), *starring Richard Widmark (with badge), was the first Hollywood film to carry the "Alan Smithee" directorial credit.* (*The Blackburn Archive*)

Juarez (1988) (TV) [Pilot episode]

Ghost Fever (1987) **Lee Madden**

I Love N. Y. (1987) **Gianni Bozzachi**

Morgan Stewart's Coming Home (1987)
Paul Aaron/Terry Windsor

Riviera (1987) (TV) [Pilot episode]
John Frankenheimer

Dalton: Code of Vengeance II (1986) (TV)

Let's Get Harry (1986) **Stuart Rosenberg**

Appointment with Fear (1985) **Razmi Thomas**

McGyver (1985) (TV) [Pilot episode]

Stitches (1985) **Rod Holcomb**

The Twilight Zone: Paladin of the Lost Hour [Episode] (1985)

Dune (1984) [TV version only] **David Lynch**

R. I. P. (1983)

Moonlight (1982)
Jackie Cooper/Rod Holcomb

Student Bodies (1981) [as producer only]
Michael Ritchie

City in Fear (1980) (TV) **Judson Taylor**

Fun and Games (1980) (TV) **Paul Bogart**

The Barking Dog (1978)

The Challenge (1970) (TV)

Death of a Gunfighter (1969)
Don Siegel/Robert Totten

Fade-In (1968) **Judson Taylor**

AFTERWORD

*B*ecause this book covers literally hundreds of titles, it's virtually impossible to verify all of the information contained herein. It is, after all, a book intended to enlighten and hopefully create a smile, not to be the definitive encyclopedia on the subject. However, we aim for accuracy, and if there's any item with which you disagree or if you have your own tale to tell about any of the movies mentioned herein, we'd certainly like to hear from you at:

Bill Givens
7510 Sunset Boulevard, #551
Los Angeles, CA 90046
Our e-mail address is bgivens@earthlink.net
Home page http://www.home.earthlink.net/~bgivens

Please contact us if you'd like to share some of your favorite Inside Jokes or just schmooze about the ones in this book. We'd love to hear from you, and perhaps a Volume II can be in the offing.

Bill Givens
Los Angeles

BIBLIOGRAPHY

Books

Boller, Paul, Jr., and Ronald L. Davis. *Hollywood Anecdotes*. New York: Ballantine Books, 1988.

Connors, Martin, and Jim Craddock, eds. *VideoHound's Golden Movie Retriever*. Detroit, MI.: Visible Ink Press, 1998.

Correy, Melinda, and George Ochoa, eds. *The Man in Lincoln's Nose*. New York: Simon & Schuster, 1990.

Givens, Bill. *Film Flubs*. Secaucus, NJ: Citadel Press, 1990.

_____. *Film Flubs: The Sequel*. Secaucus, NJ: Citadel Press, 1992.

_____. *Roman Soldiers Don't Wear Watches*. Secaucus, NJ: Citadel Press, 1996.

_____. *Son of Film Flubs*. Secaucus, NJ: Citadel Press, 1991.

Haley, Michael. *The Alfred Hitchcock Album.* Upper Saddle River, NJ: Prentice-Hall, 1981.

Harris, Robert A., and Michael S. Lasky. *The Films of Alfred Hitchcock.* Secaucus, NJ: Citadel Press, 1976.

Hay, Peter. *Movie Anecdotes.* Oxford, UK: Oxford University Press, 1990.

Maltin, Leonard et al. *Leonard Maltin's Movie & Video Guide.* New York: Penguin Putnam Group, 1997.

Robertson, Patrick. *Movie Clips.* London: Guinness Superlatives, 1989.

Rowes, Barbara. *The Book of Quotes.* New York: E. P. Dutton, 1979.

Siegel, Don. *A Siegel Film.* London: Faber and Faber, 1993.

Spencer, Donner, and Eve Page Spencer. *A Treasury of Trivia.* Saratoga, CA: Doneve Designs, 1978.

Vance, Malcom. *The Best Movie Trivia Book Ever.* New York: Bonanza Books, 1982.

Van Gelder, Peter. *That's Hollywood.* New York: HarperPerennial, 1990.

Walker, John, ed. *Halliwell's Filmgoer's & Video Viewer's Companion.* London: HarperPerennial, 1995.

Warner, Karen, and Michael Iapoce. *The Ultimate Hollywood Trivia Quiz.* San Francisco: 101 Productions, 1986.

Magazine Articles

Bojorquez, Jennifer. "Risque Frames in Roger." *Sacramento Bee,* March 31, 1994.

Bourgerol, Liz, and Nick Catoggio. "The Write Way to Act." *Entertainment Weekly*, May 9, 1997.

Dziemianowicz, Joe, and Chris Nashatawny. "See Willy." *Entertainment Weekly*, January 31, 1997.

"Filming of Disney's *Hunchback of Notre Dame*." Flashes column. *Entertainment Weekly*, July 19, 1996.

"'Filth Found in Disney Movies Is a Stretch of the Imagination." Unsigned editorial. *Omaha World Herald*, September 20, 1995.

Fink, Mitchell. "Blink During Steven Spielberg's *The Lost World*." *People*, June 16, 1997.

———. "Since Romy and Michelle's High School Reunion." *People*, June 2, 1997.

Fleming, Michael. "Jessica Rabbit Revealed." *Daily Variety*, March 14, 1994.

Givens, Bill. "Marquee Marks." *Arts & Entertainment Magazine*, March, 1992.

Goodykoontz, Bill. "Three Letters in Disney Spell 'Sin'." *Arizona Republic*, September 7, 1995.

Harvey, Steve. "Only in L.A." Various columns. *Los Angeles Times*.

Holmes, Anna, and Michael Szymankski. "Spin Control." *Entertainment Weekly*, May 24, 1996.

Horowitz, Rick. "What Would Mickey Say?" *Charleston (SC) Post and Courier*, September 11, 1995.

"How a Rumor Spread About Subliminal Sex in Disney's *Aladdin*." *Wall Street Journal*, October 24, 1995.

Karger, Dave. "Toon Time," *Entertainment Weekly*, April 3, 1998.

163

Kilday, Gregg. "To Live and Fry in L.A.," *Entertainment Weekly*, May 2, 1997.

"*Lion King* Cops Need to Get a Life." Unsigned editorial. *Wisconsin State Journal*, September 11, 1995.

Lloyd, Robert. "Without a Paddle." *LA Weekly*, January 23–29, 1998.

Manns, George. "Echo of Silence." *Entertainment Weekly*, September 8, 1995.

McCormick, Brian. "Private Jokes." *Premiere*.

"Pulp Reunion." News and Notes column. *Entertainment Weekly*, May 2, 1997.

Shull, Richard K. "From the Sublime to the Subliminal." *Indianapolis News*, September 12, 1995.

Solomon, Charles. "My Goodness, Did You Catch Those Real Guys in *Aladdin*." *Los Angeles Times*, December 6, 1992.

Stentz, Zack. Flashes column. *Entertainment Weekly*. March 20, 1998.

"10 Things You Didn't Know About Dino-Mite Movie." Unsigned column. *Globe*, June 10, 1997

Thomas, Susan Gregory. "Toontown Tricksters." *Washington Post*, March 18, 1994.

Willman, Chris. "Status of Symbol." *Entertainment Weekly*, October 6, 1996.

Internet Sources

Much of the information in this book was obtained and/or verified by an extremely comprehensive resource on the Internet, *The Internet Movie Database* (**http://www.us.imdb.com**). This database, especially the trivia section maintained by Murray Chapman (muzzle@imdb.com), contains an awesome amount of information on thousands of movies, including release dates, cast and crew lists, plot summaries, goofs, trivia, marketing information, and much more. The information is kept extremely current and its reliability is excellent. Not only is the information accessible over the Internet, but the site contains instructions allowing you to download the information and its search engines into your own computer.

Other sources include personal "fan" home pages too numerous to mention here, as well as movie-related sites, including the following:

165

The Academy Awards: **http://www.oscar.com**

Cinemania: **http://www.cinemania.msn.com**

Daily Variety: **http://www.variety.com**

The Entertainment Asylum:
http://www.asylum.com

Film.com: **http://www.film.com**

Hollywood Online: **http://www.hollywood.com**

Hollywood Reporter: **http://www.hollywood reporter.com**

MediaDome: **http://www.mediadome.com**

Mr. Showbiz: **http://www.mrshowbiz.com**

Planet Showbiz: **http://www.planetshowbiz.com**

Premiere magazine:
http://www.premieremag.com

The Remington Review:
http://www.movie-reviews.com

The Showbiz Wire: **http://www.showbizwire.com**

Siskel & Ebert: **http://www.tvplex.com/
buenavista/siskelandebert**

Studio Briefing: **http://www.newshare.com/sb/**

Some information was also obtained from contributors to various Internet newsgroups. There are thousands of newsgroups devoted to many specialized topics. Among those used as resources for this book include the following:

alt.movies

alt.movies.hitchcock

alt.movies.siskel+ebert

bit.listserve.movie.memorabilia

rec.arts.movies.current-films

rec.arts.movies.past-films

rec.arts.movies.production

rec.arts.movies.lists+surveys

rec.arts.movies.misc

An excellent resource for locating topics of interest within newsgroups can be found at **http://www.tile.net**

INDEX

171

173

ABOUT THE AUTHOR

BILL GIVENS is a Hollywood-based entertainment journalist and television writer. He is the author of seven books and a regular contributor to a variety of entertainment publications, including *Premiere, Animation, Video Software, Entertainment Weekly, People,* and *Arts & Entertainment.* He is the Hollywood correspondent for *Memphis Magazine* and is accredited by the Motion Picture Association of America as a member of the Hollywood Press Corps. His articles have been syndicated by the *New York Times Feature Syndicate* and by *Universal Features.*

He is a popular college lecturer and radio talk-show guest, and has appeared on *ABC World News, Dateline NBC, Entertainment Tonight, E!, Extra, Inside Edition, The Today Show,* as well as a number of local television programs.

After growing up in northern Mississippi, Givens spent a number of years in advertising and public relations, mainly in the Memphis, Tennessee, area. Realizing one day that, "I had never had a job that I really liked," he embarked on a freelance writing career, working for a number of local and regional publications. After obtaining his private pilot's license, he wrote his first book: *Flying with Loran-C* (1985).

In 1984, he sold his house and, realizing a dream he had since his teenage years, headed for California. Since that time he has interviewed and profiled a number of major celebrities, edited *Animation* magazine, developed segments for several entertainment-related video projects, and wrote a TV series: *Hollywood Stuntmakers*, hosted by James Coburn, for the Discovery Channel.

He is the author of five books outlining movie continuity errors, including *Film Flubs* (1990), *Son of Film Flubs* (1991), *Film Flubs: The Sequel* (1992), *Roman Soldiers Don't Wear Watches* (1996), and *Cinémato Gaffes* (1992) (France).

He was a first-place winner in the Southern Literary Festival, and his aviation book won first place, nonfiction, in the Aviation/Space Writers Award Competition.

Articles about his work have appeared in the *New York Times*, the *Los Angeles Times*, the *New York Daily News*, the *Chicago Tribune*, and the *New York Post*, as well as virtually every major market newspaper in America.

A popular radio guest, he does approximately 150 radio interviews each year, and has made repeated appearances on the British Broadcast System and on the *CBS Late, Late Radio Show with Tom Snyder and Steve Mason*.

He has a particular passion for the preservation and restoration of the nation's spectacular movie palaces, and was a founder of the Los Angeles Historic theatre Association. When he's not hanging around darkened movie theatres, he sings with the choir of All Saints' Episcopal Church, Beverly Hills, and is a member of the Communications Advisory Board of the Episcopal Diocese of Los Angeles.

Givens is listed in *Who's Who in the West*, *Who's Who in Entertainment*, and *Who's Who in the Episcopal Church*.